Enriching Ministry

Enriching Ministry

Pastoral Supervision in Practice

Edited by

Michael Paterson and Jessica Rose

scm press

© The Editors and Contributors 2014

Published in 2014 by SCM Press
Editorial office
3rd Floor
Invicta House
108–114 Golden Lane,
London
EC1Y OTG

SCM Press is an imprint of Hymns Ancient & Modern Ltd
(a registered charity)
13A Hellesdon Park Road
Norwich NR6 5DR, UK

www.scmpress.co.uk

British Library Cataloguing in Publication data

A catalogue record for this book is available
from the British Library

978 0 334 04956 2

Typeset by Regent Typesetting, London
Printed and bound by
CPI Group (UK) Ltd, Croydon

Contents

Part Two – Reflections on Practice

Part Three – Practice in Context

Part Four – The Practice of Pastoral Supervision

Acknowledgements

We recognize with gratitude all those who have entrusted their stories of professional practice to us over the years: our collaborating authors, peers, critical conversation partners, students and supervisees. We are particularly indebted to Linda Bloch, Teresa Brown, Anna Chesner, David Holt, Jane Leach, Petrina Morris, Celia Scanlan, Rachel Verney, Heather Walton and Lia Zografou without whom this book might never have been written. This volume is dedicated to Alfred Mario, who have supported and believed in us throughout this project, and to the monks and nuns of the Jerusalem Community, Rome, whose hospitality made writing possible for Michael.

About the Authors

Margaret Bazely is a pastoral counsellor and trainer, a Further Education College Chaplain and a Methodist local preacher living in Norfolk. She is a Co-Director of the Institute of Pastoral Counselling, training individuals in pastoral counselling and pastoral supervision, an Associate of the Institute of Pastoral Supervision and Reflective Practice and an accreditation assessor for the British Association for Counselling and Psychotherapy.

David Carroll is a Roman Catholic priest of the Diocese of Killaloe in Ireland and has worked as a supervisor since qualifying from the MA in Supervisory Practice course in Miltown Institute in 2007. He has worked with both individuals and groups across a broad spectrum, from people in ministry, the travelling community, teachers and those in caring professions. He has a particular interest in developing pastoral supervision for those in ministry.

Diane Clutterbuck is a presbyter, coach, supervisor and trainer, who works with clients in the UK, Ireland and Continental Europe from her base in Belfast. She is an Association of Pastoral Supervisors and Educators (APSE) accredited supervisor and educator and co-director of the Institute of Pastoral Supervision and Reflective Practice. She designs and runs courses in coaching and supervision skills for ministers and for the public and voluntary sectors.

Jane Denniston is an ordained minister in the Church of Scotland. She has been working with candidates in training for ministry since 2005 and has a particular interest in reflective practice and its significance for ministerial formation. Jane's other interests are liturgy and the theology of sexuality. Her doctoral research concerns the nature of and necessity for a pedagogical element in pastoral supervision for ministerial formation.

Linda J. Dunbar is a parish minister within the Church of Scotland and has served in Fife and Edinburgh. She is a supervisor of ministers in training and a facilitator for professional accompaniment within the Church of Scotland. She researches in the fields of the Scottish Reformation and in clergy stress.

Charles Hampton is a counselling psychologist in private practice, a senior accredited member of the British Association for Counselling and Psychotherapy (BACP) and an accredited supervisor with APSE. He has contributed to the formation and support of Anglican and Baptist clergy. He is married with children and grandchildren and relaxes with Dylan the lurcher, painting in oils and boating on the canals.

Lynette Harborne is a psychotherapist, spiritual director, supervisor and trainer working in private practice in Buckinghamshire. She has been Chair of the Association of Pastoral and Spiritual Care and Counselling, a Division of the BACP, and is also involved in the formation of clergy across denominations. She is particularly interested in the similarities and differences between psychotherapy and spiritual direction and is the author of *Psychotherapy and Spiritual Direction: Two Languages, One Voice?* (Karnac, 2012). She is currently undertaking research into the role that supervision plays in the ethical practice of spiritual direction in the United Kingdom.

Ewan Kelly is a former junior doctor, who has spent most of his working life as a healthcare chaplain and a university teacher. His experience includes chaplaincy both in two teaching hospitals and in an independent hospice. He currently works with NHS Education for Scotland on the strategic development of spiritual care and healthcare chaplaincy in NHS Scotland as Programme Director for Chaplaincy and Spiritual Care. In addition, he has a part-time position as Senior Lecturer in Pastoral Theology at the University of Edinburgh.

Ruth Layzell is a pastoral counsellor and trainer living and working in Nottingham. She is a Co-Director of the Institute of Pastoral Counselling, training individuals in pastoral counselling and pastoral supervision, an Associate of the Institute of Pastoral Supervision and Reflective Practice and Director of Training at the Sherwood Psychotherapy Institute.

Tony Nolan is a member of the Missionaries of the Sacred Heart, a religious order within the Roman Catholic tradition. He is a group facilitator, spiritual director, pastoral supervisor and trainer. Tony is a member of staff at Sarum College, Salisbury, where he is coordinator for spiritual direction, supervision and reflective practice. He also teaches reflective practice on the MA in Christian Approaches to Leadership. He is actively involved in promoting supervision and reflective practice in a wide variety of pastoral settings, such as spiritual direction, chaplaincy, pastoral and senior leadership, safeguarding and parochial ministry.

Michael Paterson is a priest, counsellor and pastoral supervisor with an extensive practice across Scotland. He is an APSE Accredited Supervisor and Trainer and Co-Director of the Institute of Pastoral Supervision and Reflective Practice. He runs training in cross-professional creative supervision and reflective practice in Edinburgh and in values-based reflective practice within the Scottish healthcare community. He is the co-author (with Jane Leach) of *Pastoral Supervision: A Handbook* (SCM Press, 2010). His doctoral research explores the persistence of grace in supervision.

Jessica Rose is a psychodynamic counsellor, pastoral supervisor and lecturer/trainer, practising in Oxford since the early 1990s. She is an accredited supervisor with APSE and an associate of the Institute of Pastoral Supervision and Reflective Practice. From 1993 to 2000 Jessica was Lecturer in Pastoral Psychology at Ripon College, Cuddesdon. She is the author of *Sharing Spaces? Prayer and the Counselling Relationship* (Darton, Longman & Todd, 2001); *Church on Trial* (Darton, Longman & Todd, 2009); *Psychology for Pastoral Contexts* (SCM Press, 2013).

Introduction

Enriching Ministry – Pastoral Supervision in Practice

MICHAEL PATERSON AND JESSICA ROSE

As anyone who has engaged in biblical studies will be aware, to avoid a reading of Scripture that is distorted for our own manipulative purposes, equal attention must be paid to:

- text,
- context and
- co-texts.

To do otherwise is to violate the sacred word. We can apply that hermeneutic principle to *Enriching Ministry – Pastoral Supervision in Practice*.

The text you hold in your hands engages people of faith in a conversation about supervision as a form of theology in practice. As such, it is underpinned by a belief in a God whose redemptive purposes are both thwarted and realized in the nitty-gritty realities of everyday pastoral life – in our attempts to care for each other, to guide and lead the communities entrusted to us, to unfold Scripture and tradition, to live lives worthy of our calling (Eph. 4.1), to foster ethical living and ultimately to set each other free (John 11.44). The text of this book rescues pastoral supervision from the charge of uncritically adopting a secular practice foreign to the kingdom culture of God's people and firmly sets it within the dialogue between theology and the social sciences (Chapter 1), in which Trinitarian relationality is key (Chapter 2) and the supervisory 'self' is embodied, intentional and incarnate

(Chapter 3). Chapter 4 reminds us of how important it is to notice and take care with our particular use of language.

Context is addressed in two ways – the general and the specific. This book arises out of a general context in which the dangers of privatized and unaccountable ministries have been exposed and in response to which pastoral workers now struggle to keep up with ministerial codes of practice, policies for safeguarding, personal and professional development plans, learning and serving covenants and so on. It also arises in response to a specific context in which training programmes have overly focused on the tasks of ministry to the neglect of those who embody those ministries. As such, it is expressive of the call to reflexivity, common across the caring professions, which find in journaling, coaching, reflective practice and supervision highly effective media for lifelong learning and ongoing personal and professional formation. While this more general context pervades the entire book, attention is also focused on the more immediate contexts of ministerial formation (Chapter 8), executive coaching (Chapter 10), spiritual direction (Chapter 11) and healthcare chaplaincy (Chapter 12).

Among the co-texts of pastoral supervision, three feature in this book:

- the overlap with line management, counselling and spiritual direction, which are explored in Chapters 5, 9 and 11;
- the practical experience and grounded wisdom of supervisees and supervisors, which find explicit voice in Chapters 5, 6, and 7;
- the growing body of literature in the field, which underpins supervisory practice and training (Chapters 1, 12 and 13).

Supervision within the caring professions: an overview of the literary co-texts

Whereas the literature in pastoral supervision is slim, its counterpart in the wider helping professions is weighty. In an address to the American Association for Theological Field Education in

1969, Thomas Klink suggested that pastoral supervision had much to learn from the practices of the wider helping professions. Not until 1977 was his suggestion taken up and the detail filled in with the publication of Kenneth Pohly's *Pastoral Supervision* in the United States and the launch of the US-based *Journal of Supervision and Training in Ministry* (now known, since 2007, as *Reflective Practice: Formation and Supervision in Ministry*).

Pohly speaks for many when he observes:

> [S]upervision is a term that is loaded with baggage. It carries an image of *bossism*, of someone in authority looking over one's shoulder and controlling every move, rewarding or punishing at will. It suggests a hierarchy of superiority/inferiority and dredges up threatening associations with the past. For this reason some people suggest abandoning the term and substituting something more palatable.[1]

Nevertheless, notwithstanding the variations in terminology and in emphasis, the literature portrays broad agreement that supervision offers an opportunity for practitioners to reflect on professional issues with one or more colleagues with a view to improving their ability to 'deliver' optimal care for those with whom they work.[2]

Within the community of faith, the term 'supervision' falls victim to what Flew coined 'death by a thousand qualifications'.[3] Croft proposes a view of 'ministry in three dimensions' in which the whole Church rather than only authorized individuals participate in *episcope* (oversight) understood as 'watching over each other in love'.[4] Pohly picks up that strand and traces the history of

---

1 K. Pohly, 2001, *Transforming the Rough Places: The Ministry of Supervision*, 2nd edn, Franklin, TN: Providence House, p. 2.

2 See, for example, P. Hawkins and R. Shohet, 2012, *Supervision in the Helping Professions*, 4th edn, Maidenhead: Open University Press; P. Cassedy, 2010, *First Steps in Clinical Supervision: A Guide for Healthcare Professionals*, Maidenhead: McGraw-Hill, Open University Press.

3 In J. Feinberg (ed.), 1968, *Reason and Responsibility: Readings in Some Basic Problems of Philosophy*, Belmont, CA: Dickenson Publishing, p. 48.

4 S. Croft, 2008, *Ministry in Three Dimensions: Ordination and Leadership in the Local Church*, revised edn, London: Darton, Longman & Todd. The Methodist

'oversight' within the covenantal relationship between God and God's people.[5] Kittel's scholarly treatise severs the traditional link between 'the offices denoted by *episkopos* in the Greek speaking world' and 'the Christian office of bishop' and helpfully outlines the use of *episcope* and its compounds in the secular and religious realms.[6]

With regard to pastoral supervision, *epeskapsato* is of particular interest as in Luke 1.68, 'God has visited (*epeskapsato*) his people and redeemed them'. Similarly, when the son of the widow of Nain is restored to life the people proclaim, 'Surely God has visited his people' (Luke 7.16). According to Kittel, 'divine visitation may carry with it a wonderful experience of grace' but 'also of judgment'.[7] In Luke 19.44 Jesus relates the time of his visitation (*kairos tes episkopes*) to his own coming to Jerusalem. *Episcope* understood as the kind of steady, reliable presence that does not shy away from assessment and judgement when required, provides pastoral supervisory practice with a solid and deeply attractive theological underpinning.

In 1902 Freud invited doctors to meet together to share observations on their experiences. The fruitfulness of these meetings resulted in his insistence a decade later that all doctors treating 'conditions of the mind' should undergo their own personal analysis as part of their training. It took a further ten years for this recommendation to become a training requirement. In 1925 supervised analysis was woven in with personal analysis and theoretical training as the third strand in psychoanalytic training. The ensuing decades saw supervision move from the 'commendable' to the 'normative' category, with the requirement in 1956 of 150 hours of supervision 'for the purpose of instruction, skill development, personal analysis and evaluation of the candidate's

---

Ordination service charges the candidate: 'These things are your common duty and delight. In them you are to watch over one another in love.' *Methodist Worship Book*, 1999, Peterborough: Methodist Publishing House, p. 302.

5 *Transforming the Rough Places*, pp. 12–13.

6 G. Kittel, 1964, *Theological Dictionary of the New Testament*, Grand Rapids, MI: Eerdmans, Vol. II, pp. 598–622.

7 Kittel, *Theological Dictionary*, Vol. II, p. 606.

development'.[8] Being rooted in the psychoanalytic tradition has left a lasting imprint upon the philosophy and practice of supervision and finds expression in two hotly contested issues within the literature:

- Who is supervision for?
- What is its focus or purpose?

Who is supervision for?

Although this question is inextricably linked to that of purpose, what makes it worth considering in its own right are the myriad assumptions that underpin the range of terms used to describe the parties involved. While the literature largely concurs in referring to the person who conducts the session as the 'supervisor', the origins of the practice within psychoanalysis can be detected in terming those on the receiving end as 'students' or 'trainees' rather than supervisees or practitioners. The significance is more than semantic since choosing to refer to the practitioner as 'trainee' or 'student' locates supervision within professional initiation processes rather than within a philosophy of lifelong learning (that is, supervision is for trainees and the professionally immature), implies a hierarchy of knowing in the relationships involved, betrays a power imbalance between the two parties – with all the concomitant ensuing dynamics that involves – and paves the way for understanding the role of supervisor in terms of assessing performance and quality control. It is interesting to note that this is the dominant understanding expressed in the literature of supervision emanating from the United States within both Clinical Pastoral Education and the caring professions at large.

---

8 Pohly, *Transforming the Rough Places*, p. 43.

What is the purpose or focus of supervision?

Turning now to the purpose or focus of supervision, Pohly asks:

> Is the aim of supervision to do therapy [to clients] *through* students, instruct students in *how* to do therapy, or provide therapy *for* students? Or is it all three of these?[9]

Supervision as 'remote' therapy or care

In the early stages of practice when novice practitioners lack confidence, it is not uncommon for them to project a medical model on to supervision and expect the supervisor to diagnose what is going on for the 'client', prescribe a remedy and dispense a treatment plan. Unconsciously, such novices regard supervision as 'remote' care. Nevertheless, while developmental stages in practitioner development are widely discussed in the literature, none of the writers supports an understanding of supervision as therapy or pastoral care at one remove.

Supervision as education

The pedagogical aim of supervision is well aired in the literature. 'The supervisor is an instructor', writes Tarachow, 'whose task it is to teach and demonstrate the theory and skills the practitioner needs to acquire competence.'[10] In the 1987 entry 'Supervision, Pastoral' in *A Dictionary of Pastoral Care*, John Millar takes a similar view: 'The Supervisor instructs by examining, framing and exploring different explanations and possibilities of what is taking place between student and client.'[11]

In more recent years the influence of educational theorists such as Dewey, Schön and Kolb is acknowledged and clearly detectable

---

9 Pohly, *Transforming the Rough Places*, p. 44; emphasis in the original.

10 S. Tarachow, 1963, *An Introduction to Psychotherapy*, New York: International Universities Press, p. 15.

11 J. P. Millar, 'Supervision, Pastoral', in A. V. Campbell, 1987, *A Dictionary of Pastoral Care*, London: SPCK, p. 273.

in writers who fundamentally understand supervision as a learning environment. More particularly, the psychoanalyst Donald Winnicott's notion of a space in which a child feels safe enough to play is widely taken up by writers who emphasize the importance of supervision as a space conducive to learning,[12] a space for creative play[13] and a space for integrative learning.[14] Most of the published models identify the capacity for learning inherent in supervision. Thus, Michael Carroll sees supervision as a 'learning relationship' and names 'teaching' the second of his seven tasks of supervision, Kadushin speaks of the 'educative' function, Proctor the 'formative' task and Hawkins the 'developmental' function of supervision.

Supervision as transformation

Pohly's third question, 'is the aim of supervision to provide therapy *for* students?' receives a clear 'no' in the literature. While many writers acknowledge the inevitable effect on one's personal life of bearing witness to countless tales of suffering and human exigencies, the literature concurs in asserting that only material which arises in response to the client's story or impacts upon the ability to 'stay with' the client has a place in supervision. Other material belongs in personal counselling, spiritual direction or line management.

Nevertheless, the literature shows an increasing awareness of the therapeutic benefits of supervision for the practitioner without it losing its client or other centredness. Foskett and Lyall are among those who underscore the value of a regular space in which integration of self, practice and world view can take place.[15] Recent years have seen a flurry of new books which go one stage

---

12 For example, F. Ward, 2005, *Lifelong Learning: Theological Education and Supervision*, London: SCM Press, p. 88.

13 G. Bolton, 2003, *Reflective Practice: Writing and Professional Development*, London and Thousand Oaks, CA: Sage, p. 33; C. Schuck, C. and J. Wood, 2011, *Inspiring Creative Supervision*, London and Philadelphia: Jessica Kingsley, pp. 53–84.

14 J. Foskett and D. Lyall, 1988, *Helping the Helpers: Supervision in Pastoral Care*, London: SPCK, p. 114.

15 Foskett and Lyall, *Helping the Helpers*, p. 114.

further and speak of the transformative impulse of supervision.[16] Underlying that transformative impulse are three things:

- an emphasis on relationship as a catalyst for transformational learning;
- an awareness that the acquisition of skills and competences do not of themselves make someone a good practitioner;
- an agreement that practitioners need to become clear who they are in order to ensure that in making intentional use of the self their 'professional actions' remain 'aligned with personal beliefs and values'.[17]

From therapeutic to pastoral supervision

So far we have traced the psychotherapeutic roots of supervision, explored the *telos* of the practice and critically evaluated unspoken assumptions. In so doing we agree with Ward that the therapeutic literature 'has offered useful insights to theologians and reflective practitioners'.[18] Nevertheless, using the analogy of a swimming pool, we are anxious to ensure that the deep end of enquiry is not ceded to the world of the psychological therapies, while theology and the practices of faith communities are consigned to swim 'in the shallow end of meaning'.[19] Thus, with Ward, we want 'to locate the work of supervision more centrally within a learning church and the ministry it offers in today's world'.[20] To that end we now turn to issues of theological significance.

16 Among these are M. Carroll and M. Gilbert, 2011, *On Being a Supervisee: Creating Learning Partnerships*, 2nd edn, London: Vukani Publishing, pp. 22–7; R. Shohet (ed.), 2011, *Supervision as Transformation: A Passion for Learning*, London and Philadelphia: Jessica Kingsley, pp. 146–60; N. Weld, 2012, *A Practical Guide to Transformative Supervision for the Helping Professions: Amplifying Insight*, London: Jessica Kingsley, pp. 19–28.

17 D. Somerville and J. Keeling, 2004, 'A Practical Approach to Promote Reflective Practice within Nursing', *Nursing Times*, 100:12, p. 42.

18 Ward, *Lifelong Learning*, p. 5.

19 'The deep end of "truth" has been ceded to science, while theology swims in the shallow end of "meaning".' R. Reno, 2000, 'The Radical Orthodoxy Project', *First Things: A Monthly Journal of Religion and Public Life*, February, p. 37.

20 Ward, *Lifelong Learning*, p. 5.

PART ONE

Theological and Philosophical Perspectives

I

Pastoral Supervision: From Therapeutic Leftovers to Public Theology

MICHAEL PATERSON

In this chapter we will explore the relationship between Practical Theology and the Social Sciences and identify understandings of supervision inherited from the wider caring professions. The second half of the chapter outlines the unique hallmarks of pastoral supervision as a form of public theology that is vocational, contemplative, vision-focused, spacious, redemptive and sabbatical. The chapter concludes by sketching the capacity for vocational regeneration inherent in pastoral supervision.

Eleven years after Pohly published his book *Pastoral Supervision* in the United States (in 1977), the term 'pastoral supervision' first appeared in print in the UK, in Foskett and Lyall's *Helping the Helpers: Supervision and Pastoral Care* (1988). In the Preface the authors laid no claim to new wisdom about what they describe as 'a concept and a practice which has been extensively discussed in other contexts'. Nevertheless, they 'write from within the context of faith, believing that "pastoral supervision" raises questions peculiar to itself, especially in relation to the dialogue between Christian faith and the human sciences'.[1] Thus, they place pastoral supervision within the dialogue between faith and the human sciences. Why? Because of the inescapable relationship between the

---

1 J. Foskett and D. Lyall, 1988, *Helping the Helpers: Supervision in Pastoral Care*, London: SPCK, p. ix.

practice of pastoral supervision as public theology and the disciplines of psychology and contextual analysis that inform it.

In exploring this relationship, we will use Paul Tillich's 'method of correlation', whereby insights from Christian revelation are correlated with those from philosophy and psychology.

Paul Tillich

Paul Tillich (1886–1965) was the German Protestant theologian par excellence, who has 'come to represent the requirement to take culture with utmost seriousness when articulating theology'.[2] In response to the crisis of the First and, especially, the Second World Wars, Tillich placed liberal theology in the dock and found it wanting. Having fled from Nazi Germany to the United States he wrote:

> Only those who have experienced the shock of transitoriness, the anxiety in which they are aware of their finitude, the threat of non-being, can understand what the notion of God means. Only those who have experienced the tragic ambiguities of our historical existence and have totally questioned the meaning of existence can understand what the symbol of the Kingdom of God means.[3]

Against that backdrop,

> in using the method of correlation, systematic theology proceeds in the following way: it makes an analysis of the human

---

2 H. Walton, 2007, *Imagining Theology: Women, Writing and God*, London: T. & T. Clark, p. 53.

3 *Systematic Theology I*, 1953, cited in E. Graham, H. Walton and F. Ward, 2007, *Theological Reflection: Sources*, London: SCM Press, p. 154. Against the backdrop of the Holocaust, Rabbi Irving Greenberg makes a similar point: 'No statement, theological or otherwise should be made, that would not be credible in the presence of burning children.' I. Greenberg, 1977, 'Cloud of Smoke, Pillar of Fire: Judaism, Christianity and Modernity after the Holocaust', in E. Fleischner (ed.), *Auschwitz: Beginning of a New Era?*, New York: KTAV, p. 23.

situation out of which the existential questions arise and it demonstrates that the symbols used in the Christian message are the answers to these questions.[4]

Through his engagement with the New York Psychology group, Tillich saw the dialogue between Christianity and psychology as an important and specific example of the method of correlation. In the emerging therapeutic vocabulary of guilt, freedom, catharsis and repression he discerned clear echoes of the biblical notions of sin, grace and forgiveness.

According to Graham, Walton et al., Tillich

> regarded [therapeutic vocabulary] as contemporary expressions of enduring human dilemmas to which the gospel offers definitive answers [and] concluded that there was an essential continuity and convergence between the language of psychotherapy and the language of faith and that the activities of counselling and therapy were akin to the functions of traditional pastoral care in creating and implementing 'the good news of acceptance'.[5]

However, in contrast to the humanistic school of psychotherapy which advocates the human capacity for self-actualization, Tillich reveals his theological conservatism in asserting the primacy of theology over culture in seeing psychotherapy, as 'a sort of "prelude" to the Divine or ultimate'.[6]

The apologetic and dialectical aspects of correlation

Correlation did not begin with Tillich. There has been a wide range of understanding, emphasis and evaluation of the term across the centuries. Broadly speaking it encompasses two dimensions, both

---

4 Cited in J. Swinton and H. Mowat, 2006, *Practical Theology and Qualitative Research*, London: SCM Press, p. 77.

5 Graham, Walton et al., *Theological Reflection: Sources*, p. 155.

6 Graham, Walton et al., *Theological Reflection: Sources*, p. 156.

of which can be traced in Christian history: the 'apologetic' and the 'dialectical'.

The 'apologetic' dimension of correlation is seen where faith engages with the surrounding culture. An early example is 2 Kings 18—19, where the besieged people employ Aramaic for political negotiations with Assyrian imperial power (the conversation 'on the city wall') and Hebrew to explore faith, prayer and prophecy in the conversation 'behind the wall'. Walter Brueggemann highlights the importance of the conversation 'behind the wall' in shaping the conversation 'on the wall'. He advocates the place of 'disciplined conversation' in the grammar and syntax of the Christian community 'in order that it be free, energized and faithful in the public conversation necessarily conducted in other categories'.[7] Another example is Paul using the altar to an unknown God in Athens to introduce his hearers to Christianity (Acts 17.16–33).

Throughout Christian history we find different forms of apologetic correlation: the second-century Apologists' engagement with Greek philosophy, Arius' sea shanties concerning the nature of Christ, composed in the third century as a form of catechesis, Thomas Aquinas' synthesis of theology with Aristotelian philosophy, Hans Küng's insistence on a critical *confrontation* between Jesus and contemporary reality, the Second Vatican Council's Pastoral Constitution on the Church in the Modern World and Pope Paul VI's Apostolic Exhortation on Evangelization in the Modern World, which committed the Catholic Church to read the signs of the times as a prelude to the 'new evangelization'.

The dialectical dimension of correlation, on the other hand, creates a dialogue between theology and the surrounding culture in which theology itself is invited to change and grow. We can find many examples among the theologians of the twentieth and twenty-first centuries:

---

7 W. Brueggemann, 1991, '2 Kings 18—19: The Legitimacy of a Sectarian Hermeneutic: Interpretation and Obedience', in *Interpretation and Obedience*, Minneapolis: Fortress Press, pp. 41–69.

- Ernst Troeltsch, who pioneered the sociology of religion and gave primacy to sociology in questions of theology;[8]
- Dietrich Bonhoeffer and Reinhold Niebuhr, who drew on sociology in so far as it was able to shed light on the theological project;[9]
- Paul Tillich
- Edward Schillebeeckx, who, in contrast to Tillich, regarded human experience as a *source* of theology and called for a critical correlation and at times 'confrontation' between Christian tradition and present-day experiences;[10]
- Edward Farley, who spoke of the 'mutual absorption' of theology and the social sciences;[11]
- Rosemary Radford Ruether, who expanded the horizons of correlation to include what she calls 'the prophetic principle'.[12]

In spite of the differences between the apologetic and dialectical dimensions of the correlative method, there is common ground between the two:

- an emphasis on the value of the conversation between theology and contemporary experience;
- an understanding of how Christian theory and practice change and develop through what Graham et al. call 'an open exchange

---

8 M. D. Chapman, 2001, *Ernst Troeltsch and Liberal Theology: Religion and Cultural Synthesis in Wilhelmine Germany*, New York: Oxford University Press; S. C. Barton, 2005, 'Social-Scientific Criticism: Definition and Description', in K. J. Vanhoozer, C. G. Bartholomew, D. J. Treier, N. T. Wright (eds), 2005, *Dictionary for Theological Interpretation of the Bible*, London: SPCK, pp. 753–5.

9 R. H. Roberts, 2005, *Religion, Theology and the Human Sciences*, Cambridge: Cambridge University Press, pp. 375–7.

10 Cited in F. Schüssler Fiorenza and J. P. Gavin (eds), 2011, *Systematic Theology: Roman Catholic Perspectives*, 2nd edn, Minneapolis: Fortress Press, pp. 42–3.

11 Roberts, *Religion, Theology and the Human Sciences*, p. 377.

12 R. R. Ruether, 1985, 'Feminist Interpretation: A Method of Correlation', in L. M. Russell (ed.), *Feminist Interpretation of the Bible*, Philadelphia: Westminster Press, pp. 111–24. In citing Rosemary Radford Reuther as an exemplar of liberation theology, I intentionally refuse the reductionism that would consider her contribution exclusively within feminist theology, since I consider the latter an instance of the former. See too Fiorenza and Gavin (eds), *Systematic Theology*, p. 45.

of ideas and debate with different cultural disciplines, values, images and world-views';[13]

- the belief that grace and truth kiss and embrace (Psalm 85.10) beyond the walls erected around Christian revelation by the Church.

There are, of course, those who question the usefulness of any dialogue between theology and the social sciences. Three such dissonant voices can be heard in the Christian tradition:

- Christian fundamentalists for whom belief 'is seen as a "bulwark" against contemporary philosophy and criticism';[14]
- theologians of the Christian East for whom the Enlightenment and modernity simply have not happened;[15]
- the Radical Orthodoxy movement, which holds that 'faith evacuates philosophy' or that 'the whole world is fit for absorption into a theological framework'.[16]

Given, however, the mutual dependency between theology and psychology which characterizes pastoral supervision, we shall take a form of Tillich's method known as critical correlation as a basic tool for exploring the relationship between theology and psychology as it relates to supervision in a pastoral context.

Critical correlation

The debate about whether theology, as Tillich believed, remains primary in the relationship continues today. In her book, *Theology and Pastoral Counselling: A New Interdisciplinary Approach*,

---

13 Graham, Walton et al., *Theological Reflection: Sources*, p. 138.

14 K. Berding, 2003, 'The Hermeneutical Framework of Social-Scientific Criticism: How Much Can Evangelicals Get Involved?, *The Evangelical Quarterly* 75:1, p. 6.

15 See, for example, V. Lossky, 1976, *The Mystical Theology of the Eastern Church*, New York: St Vladimir's Press, p. 42.

16 J. Sharlet, 2000, 'Theologians Seek to Reclaim the World with God and Postmodernism', *The Chronicle of Higher Education* (June 23), p. 22; R. R. Reno, 2000, 'The Radical Orthodoxy Project', *First Things: A Monthly Journal of Religion and Public Life*, February, p. 40.

Deborah van Deusen Hunsinger explores the choice between the Barthian view 'that sees theology and psychology as two distinct discourses' and the view exemplified by theologians such as Thomas Oden who, in 'seeking an integration' between them 'collapse the differences'.[17] In defining the relationship between theology and psychology, van Deusen Hunsinger draws on the discussions held at the Council of Chalcedon in 451 CE about the divinity and humanity of Christ. At Chalcedon it was agreed that he is both human *and* divine without confusion, change, separation or division. Van Deusen Hunsinger suggests that the relationship between theology and pastoral counselling can be seen as similar to that between the two natures of Christ.

Just as in Christ, divinity and humanity are related without confusion or change so, by extension, Hunsinger argues, the twin disciplines of theology and the social sciences have 'specific roles to play' and 'reveal specific forms of knowledge which should not be confused with each other'. Following Barth, she holds that while 'theology can identify itself with psychology, psychology does not have the power to identify itself with theology'.[18] What results is a complex and rather forced parallel process in which she sees the co-inherence of the divinity and humanity of Christ played out in the relationship, 'without separation or division' (as in the Chalcedonian formula) between theology and the social sciences.

Among Barthians, Hunsinger's book has received considerable acclaim. I myself remain unconvinced: in the tug of war between theology and the social sciences, her scheme has predestined that theology will always win. Such an a priori 'applied theology' stance will hardly set theology free from what Stephen Pattison calls its 'dusty academic bondage',[19] far less offer 'critical correctives to the failures and distortions of Christian history'.[20]

---

17 B. J. Miller-McLemore, 1998, 'Review of *Theology and Pastoral Counseling: A New Interdisciplinary Approach*', *Pastoral Psychology* 46:4, p. 301.

18 Swinton and Mowat, *Practical Theology and Qualitative Research*, p. 85.

19 S. Pattison, 2000, 'Some Straw for the Bricks: A Basic Introduction to Theological Reflection', in J. Woodward and S. Pattison (eds), *The Blackwell Reader in Pastoral and Practical Theology*, Oxford: Blackwell p. 137.

20 Graham, Walton et al., *Theological Reflection: Sources*, p. 138.

Critical correlation goes beyond this stance. The result is strikingly described by the Scottish theologian Duncan Forrester: 'Public theology is not the in-house chatter or domestic housekeeping of a sect concerned above all with its own inner life and little interest in what goes on outside.'[21] Feminist and Queer theologians go further in seeing the transformative potential of correlation on the basis, as Rebecca Chopp puts it, that 'extratheological sources and insights are often necessary as critical correctives to the failures and distortions of Christian history'.[22]

If critical correlation began as a pebble tossed into an academic pond, its ripples have ensured a tsunami in the thinking and practice of theology across the globe. In South American favelas and in Asian shanty towns, in the lives of women who have been 'heard into speech'[23] and in gay men and women who have escaped the 'narrow coffin world of the closet'[24] and increasingly in theology's turn towards a concern for global and ecological issues, critical correlative approaches to theology have helped roll away the stone from entombed lives and encouraged God's people to 'connect the prose and the passion' of contemporary living.[25] In so doing, critical correlation has emancipated theology from the exclusive hands of the literate and educationally privileged and restored it to its homeland 'in the middle of human history and experience'.[26]

---

21 D. Forrester, 2000, *Truthful Action: Explorations in Practical Theology*, London: T. & T. Clark, p. 127.

22 R. S. Chopp, 2005, 'Feminist and Womanist Theologies', in D. F. Ford with R. Muers (ed.), *The Modern Theologians*, 3rd edn, Oxford: Blackwell, p. 393; Graham, Walton et al., *Theological Reflection: Sources*, p. 138.

23 N. Morton, 1985, *The Journey is Home*, Boston: Beacon.

24 P. Monette, 1992, *Becoming a Man: Half a Life Story*, New York: Harcourt Brace Jovanovich, p. 2.

25 'Only connect the prose and the passion, and both will be exalted, and human love will be seen at its highest. Live in fragments no longer', E. M. Forster, *Howard's End*, chapter 22.

26 Cf. J. McDade, 1991, 'Catholic Theology in the Post-Conciliar Period', in A. Hastings (ed.), *Modern Catholicism*, London: SPCK, pp. 423–4; H. J. Gagey, 2010, 'Pastoral Theology as a Theological Project', in J. Sweeney, G. Simmonds and D. Lonsdale (eds), *Keeping Faith in Practice: Aspects of Catholic Pastoral Theology*, London: SCM Press, pp. 80–98.

Nevertheless, critical correlation raises as many questions as it answers. For example, if we are to avoid the reductionism of 'applied theology' or 'applied psychology' and eliminate the risk of splitting theology from practice, we need to consider what weight should be given to theology and to the insights of the social sciences when considering an issue facing an individual or society today. Should the balance of the scales be tipped in either direction? And in the dialogue between theology and the social sciences, what counts as 'normative', human experience or divine revelation? Again with Swinton and Mowat we may indeed ask:

> Can the social sciences *really* challenge theology at a fundamental level as the implications of this [correlative] method suggest? *How can a system of knowledge created by human beings challenge a system of knowledge that claims to be given by God?*[27]

Yet, that to me is the glorious task entrusted to the Church by Christ in the post-resurrection age between the Ascension and the Parousia.

While it is true that we cannot expect the social sciences to answer theological questions, we must also recognize that critical correlation offers an escape tunnel from what Forrester describes as 'the in-house language of a ghetto which has hardly any lines of communication open to the outside world'.[28] In this way the theological task is no longer focused on solving the problems of individuals so much as on interpreting the communities (including their social and political structures) in which those individuals live and in which those problems arise.

Rather than fostering pious and unrealistic forms of theological reflection, Stephen Pattison is right to suggest that it is 'much more honest, perhaps, to acknowledge that there are enormous gaps between some situations in the contemporary world and the religious tradition' while 'maintain[ing] the belief that theological

---

27 Swinton and Mowat, *Practical Theology and Qualitative Research*, p. 83; emphasis in the original.
28 Forrester, *Truthful Action*, p. 62.

reflection understood as active enquiry is as much about exploring and living with gaps as well as with similarities'. The panoply of liberation theologies that have sprung up in the last century underscore Pattison's thesis that 'we need to get used to the idea that theologies can be disposable and contextual and need not be relevant at all times and in all places and they may, indeed, be thoroughly idiosyncratic'.[29]

Given the vagaries of human nature, not to mention the social and political realities operative in any given pastoral situation, pastoral supervision offers an invaluable opportunity for 'theologically rich, psychologically informed, contextually sensitive'[30] exploration in which the inevitable friction that arises in the gap between the kingdom of God and pastoral life can be aired, shared, received and reframed in a hospitable environment.

The hallmarks of a theology of pastoral supervision

Since pastoral supervision is still fairly new on the UK pastoral scene, it is not surprising that people of faith have sometimes uncritically adopted ways of working the genesis and context of which arise from communities of practice with differing value systems and end goals. Yet, if ministers are to be 'sustained from the inside'[31] in their leadership and service of God's people, surely what is needed is something bespoke and fit for purpose that weaves together the very best of what is 'out there' (in the practices of social workers, counsellors, nurses) with our own distinctive spiritual and theological values. Conscious of the danger of shoehorning a new practice into an old theological paradigm, I have resisted the temptation to outline a theology *of* supervision and instead want to identify some of the characteristics which I consider crucial to such a project. Supervision is:

---

29 Pattison, 'Some Straw for the Bricks', p. 143.

30 From the definition of pastoral supervision of the Association of Pastoral Supervisors and Educators (APSE): www.pastoralsupervision.org.uk

31 Oriah Mountaindreamer, 1999, *The Invitation*, San Francisco: HarperOne.

- vocational
- contemplative
- vision-focused
- spacious
- redemptive
- sabbatical.

Supervision is vocational

In addition to what every other caring group attends to in supervision, a bespoke tailored approach needs to take seriously that what people of faith expend their time and energy on is not just a job but a vocation, a response to a sense of calling. Rowan Williams writes of vocation in striking terms:

> Here at least, whatever the cost, I am in the truth. Anything else would be playing, messing around with a tame reality I could control, and reality is not like that. Vocation is, you could say, what's left when all the games have stopped. It's that elusive residue that we are here to discover, and to help one another to discover.[32]

Supervision becomes pastoral and theological when it not only permits but explicitly invites exploration of how that vocation is being lived out in practice. Supervision, understood as a place where the games have stopped and the truth can be told, offers an invaluable opportunity for rediscovering the glory of our calling and for promoting personal, professional and spiritual integration, freedom and identity.

Supervision is contemplative

In a culture plagued by the gods of efficiency and productivity, supervision is pastoral in character when it looks beneath the

---

32 R. Williams, 2002, *Open to Judgement*, London: Darton, Longman & Todd.

busy-ness of daily activities to the spiritual practices that under-pin and sustain our lives: prayer, meditation, holy reading, holy looking, silence and nourishing spiritual conversation. The con-templative character of reflection is engendered when we put down the tools of our respective trades to 'stare into the distance ... before bending again to [our] labour'.[33]

Supervision is vision-focused

As an invitation to attend to the vision that shapes my identity, supervision invites me to name the core beliefs and values that inform my understanding of my role in the workplace and to engage in a courageous dialogue between those aspects of my role that sit well with my personal vision and those that clash; between the parts of my role that I accept and the parts that I reject; between the skills and vulnerabilities of which I am aware and those of which I am blind. With eyes wide open, such reflec-tion invites congruence, balance and harmony between inner and outer worlds.

Supervision is spacious

Nothing does more to kill the fresh creative air of supervision than an urgent sense that the clock is ticking, that something (worse still 'someone') has to be fixed and that a riddle requires reso-lution. Mark Stobert writes of the spaciousness needed in ministry and (by extension) in subsequent reflection:

> The slow, slow questions wait
>   In hiding.
> They wait until they perceive that
> Once exposed in the open they
> Won't be dropped or damaged.

---

33 'The Wires of the Night', Billy Collins, 2002, *Sailing Alone around the Room*, New York: Random House, pp. 121–2.

Even a space (opened) between will suffice
  Only after delicate testing ...

The reply? Ah! The slow, slow, slower answers
  Reach and embrace the questions,
  Not with words
Not in song
  But as dance
The dance of love.[34]

Supervision is redemptive

In a book on caring for the carers, Jon Conte says that just as 'oil splatters on the painter's shirt or dirt gets under the gardener's nails' so the work we do 'leaves its mark upon us and has an impact'.[35] It goes without saying that the ministries in which we are engaged impact greatly upon us. Sometimes they bring out the best in us. At other times we fall short of our own or other people's expectations. Being able to expose those shortfalls to the loving and supportive eye of another can go a long way to releasing ourselves from the limitations of being human, dusting ourselves down and getting up to face a new day. But that takes courage and asks us to admit our own neediness. Brian Patten could be speaking of the redemptive characteristic of supervision when he writes:

And the one throwing the lifebelt
Even he needs help at times;
Stranded on the beach
Terrified of the waves.[36]

---

34 Mark Stobert, private communication, used with his permission.

35 Cited in L. van Dernoot Lipsky, 2009, *Trauma Stewardship: An Everyday Guide to Caring for Self while Caring for Others*, San Francisco: Berrett-Koehler Publishers, p. xii.

36 Brian Patten, 'Throwing the Lifebelt', permission sought.

Supervision is sabbatical

Supervision that is fit for purpose for people of faith should have a sabbatical quality about it. Engaging in supervision should offer people sufficient rest to enable them to return to work renewed, energized and refreshed. Sonya Rose's 'Eighth Day' captures this quality of reflective practice beautifully:

I declare today
the eighth day of the week,
freed of oughts and shoulds and even musts;
a holiday, a holy day,
a gift without strings,
a time-space to savour,
to expand into rooms long neglected
and linger there,
patiently,
watching for unknown buds to flower –
Welcome them,
though they may startle
with dark,
unexpected blooms.[37]

As an eighth-day activity, 'freed of oughts and shoulds and even musts', pastoral supervision 'expands into rooms long neglected, and lingers there, patiently, watching for unknown buds to flower … with dark, unexpected blooms'.

Pastoral supervision and vocational regeneration

The demands of contemporary ministry would have been inconceivable to our forebears a century ago. The requirements of inspection, accountability, risk assessment and litigation have all contributed to 'a world gone mad with speed, potential and choice, [in which] we continually overestimate what we can do,

---

37 Sonya Rose, in Poems in the Waiting Room, August 2008; permission granted.

build, fix, care for or make happen in one day'.[38] As a result, many in ministry report feeling buffeted about by strong and unpredictable currents. Renzenbrink describes how

[f]or many of us, the elaborate architecture we build around our hearts begins to resemble a fortress. We build up our defences, we add a moat, we throw in some crocodiles, we forge more weapons, we build higher and higher walls. Sooner or later, we find ourselves locked in by the very defences we have constructed for our own protection. We will find the key to our liberation only when we accept what we once did to survive is now destroying us. And thus we begin the work of dismantling our fortress, releasing the crocodiles back to their habitat, and melting down the weapons to recycle into ploughshares.[39]

This is hardly surprising since nowhere are ontology (inhabiting the being of a profession) and epistemology (how we arrive at 'knowing' what to do and how to act) more clearly wedded together in an indissoluble bond than in the life of those who minister and whose tools of the trade are nothing less than the intentional use of the self.[40] After all, 'who else, with nothing in their hands, deals day in day out with the crushed, the bruised and the defeated?'[41] After thirty plus years in ministry I recognize myself in van Dernoot Lipsky's honest admission:

After years of bearing witness to others' suffering, I finally came to understand that my exposure had changed me on a fundamental level. There had been an osmosis: I had absorbed and accumulated [distress] to the point that it had become a

---

38 W. Muller, 2010, *A Life of Being, Having, and Doing Enough*, New York: Harmony Books, p. 5.

39 I. Renzenbrink, 2011, *Caregiver Stress and Staff Support in Illness, Dying and Bereavement*, Oxford: Oxford University Press, pp. 43–4.

40 Cf. E. Kelly, 2012, *Personhood and Presence: Self as a Resource for Spiritual and Pastoral Care*, London: Continuum.

41 Derek Fraser, in his opening remarks at the 'Enhancing Quality and Reducing Costs: An Evidence Approach' conference, 12 March 2012, Beardmore Hotel, Clydebank.

part of me, and my view of the world had changed. I realized eventually that I had come into my work armed with a burning passion and a tremendous commitment but few other internal resources. As you know, there is a time for fire, but what sustains the heat – for the long haul – is the coals. And coals I had none of. I did the work for a long time with very little ability to integrate my experiences emotionally, cognitively, spiritually or physically.[42]

My experience of supervising clergy over the last decade has convinced me that when supervision is truly pastoral (both in its care for the carer and in its attention to the missiological and kingdom tasks which characterize the encounter), the 'heat' of ministry can indeed be sustained by regularly 'coming away by ourselves to a quiet place' (cf. Mark 6.31) in which we reconnect with those 'elemental stories' which motivate us[43] and courageously face the gap between who we espouse to be and what we actually do. Pastoral supervision, understood as the place where we attend, monitor and tweak the internal wiring that directs our ministerial reflexes and impulses, is of deep personal and ecclesial significance. In words that give expression to Pohly's covenantal character of supervision, Williams writes:

> I have no right to destroy your vision, nor you, mine. I have no business to devalue your understanding or make light of your struggles, nor you, mine. But we have the right – and perhaps the duty – to put the questions to each other and hear them from each other.[44]

---

42 Van Dernoot Lipsky, *Trauma Stewardship*, pp. 3–4. Hawkins and Chesterman make a similar point in the context of teaching: 'Most teachers enter the profession passionate about their work, keen to make a contribution and experiencing the work as personally developmental. By mid-career, many of these same teachers are finding their work a chore, have lost the joy of teaching and have stopped learning and developing.' P. Hawkins and D. Chesterman, 2006, *Every Teacher Matters*, London: Teacher Support Network, p. 24.

43 S. Ryan, 2004, *Vital Practice: Stories from the Healing Arts, the Homeopathic and Supervisory Way*, Portland, OR: Sea Change, p. 8.

44 Williams, *Open to Judgement*, p. 110.

Pastoral supervision offers an opportunity for that mutual vocational questioning.

Summary and conclusions

In this chapter I have adopted a critical correlation approach which values the contribution of psychotherapy and social analysis to the supervisory space. While I share Pohly's view that 'pastoral supervision at its best is an integrative art, drawing upon the wide range of resources',[45] I am convinced with J. C. Karl that

> in a time of spiritual hunger and institutional deterioration, pastoral counsellors [and by extension pastoral supervisors] have an important mission to demonstrate that the 'rejected stone' of spirituality may indeed be the 'cornerstone' of environments that sustain practitioners and serve people well.[46]

In arguing for supervision as a place where personal vocation comes face to face with ministerial practice (understood as the unfolding of that vocation in action) I am advocating the need for a conversation 'behind the wall' (2 Kings 18—19). With Brueggemann I am concerned that in turning uncritically and too readily to counselling or business management for insight, 'we have forgotten our primal language. Other languages take its place.'[47] But far from joining Milbank in declaring engagement with the social sciences questionable or of aligning myself with Tillich or Hunsinger in their prioritization of theology, I stand with David F. Ford in advocating a theology not of withdrawal but of immersion 'in the contingencies, complexities and ambiguities

---

45 K. Pohly, 2001, *Transforming the Rough Places: The Ministry of Supervision*, 2nd edn, Franklin, TN: Providence House, p. 23.

46 J. C. Karl, 1998, 'Discovering Spiritual Patterns: Including Spirituality in Staff Development and the Delivery of Psychotherapy Services', *American Journal of Pastoral Counseling* 1:4, p. 22.

47 Brueggemann, '2 Kings 18—19', p. 42.

of creation and history', which 'seeks to do justice to many contexts, levels, voices, moods, genres, systems and responsibilities'.[48]

'Theologically rich, psychologically informed, contextually sensitive' supervision[49] has the potential to do just that in creating a space to which the whole of oneself can come and in which truth-telling is practised. The time has passed for uncritically baptizing existing practices with the liberal sprinkling of Christian piety and sentiment. If pastoral supervision is to be theologically and psychologically bilingual, then narrative identity, Christian anthropology and psychological frames of understanding must all be painstakingly picked over with equal and unbiased care.

---

48 Ford with Muers (ed.), *The Modern Theologians*, p. 761.

49 Association of Pastoral Supervisors and Educators definition of Pastoral Supervision, 2008: www.pastoralsupervision.org.uk

2

Rooted and Grounded in Love: A Theological Framework for Pastoral Supervision

JESSICA ROSE

This chapter is based on a talk given as the keynote address to the 2012 conference of the Association of Pastoral Supervisors and Educators (APSE) (www.pastoralsupervision.org.uk). It introduces a framework for thinking about supervision based on two key Christian concepts, Trinity and Incarnation, and explores the place of the supervisory relationship in a community of faith.

In Chapter 1, Michael Paterson has outlined the uses and pitfalls of correlating insights from theology with those from the social sciences. Here, I will not be attempting a correlation between theology and psychology so much as using the Christian concepts of Trinity and Incarnation to provide a framework for thinking about pastoral supervision. The aim is to encourage a mutual appreciation between two practical disciplines – theology and psychology – that are both essential in pastoral supervision but that often have difficulty being polite to each other. As bedfellows they can be rather like two people in a volatile but successful marriage: the strengths of one partner are mirrored by the weakness of the other and vice versa.

To put it crudely, if we lean too much on theology, we can become psychologically lazy, relying on God to sort out all our problems or taking a restricted view of human beings that does not take life as it is lived into account; and if we start from psychology, there is a danger of leaving God out of it altogether. All too often psychologists assume that religious belief – often poorly understood – is problematic if not pathological. Yet, a psychology that cuts itself off from the world of spirit also cuts itself off from vast areas of human experience, even though it does not need to take theology into account in order to be useful in its own terms.

On the other hand, a theology that is not rooted in the givenness of human nature will not be able to integrate psychology and will therefore be of little use to us in daily life. Sadly, religious language is frequently used to bypass the work that needs to be done at a psychological level in processing experience, for example in moving too quickly to forgive an injury, or ascribing life's difficulties to demonic attack rather than being prepared to look at how one might oneself be contributing to what is going on. 'God-talk' can also be a way of avoiding uncomfortable truths about human behaviour. Yet, by definition, theology as the study of God will always be incomplete, since we will never be able to give a total description of God or God's relation to the world. It must, then, be open to learning from new ways of understanding the world – which is itself a revelation of God's creative energy.

As time goes on, the gap between these two disciplines is unlikely to disappear. It is probably not even desirable that it should, but perhaps we may go some way to *bridging* the gap. As with the couple in the volatile marriage, however, we need to take the advice so often heard on the London Underground, and *mind* the gap as well. It may not be possible to integrate theology and psychology completely, but we might make some progress towards what in pastoral supervision we could call 'joined-up practice'.

The 'gap': some differences between pastoral care and psychological therapies

Pastoral care has a vast scope. At one end of the scale it might mean fetching in shopping or offering someone a cup of tea; it could be helping homeless people, working with young people or hospital visiting; or it might involve doing in-depth work with someone at the very heart of their life story. An act of pastoral care might last for two minutes or for several years.

Furthermore, pastoral care is often (though not always) mutual. It takes place in a community where people care for each other. Unlike psychotherapy or counselling, pastoral care is essentially community based and gospel driven. It is also a very human activity – as magnificent sometimes in its generosity and outpouring of love as it is dogged by unconscious need, power play, burnout and all those things where supervision can be helpful. And it is also rooted in an understanding of human beings as loved by God and created in God's image: 'Just as you did it to one of the least of these ... you did it to me' (Matt. 25.40).

Pastoral supervisors with a background in therapy or counselling bring to this fertile chaos insights and techniques generally informed by psychological frameworks for understanding how human beings tick. Broadly these fall into three kinds, all of which can enable people to grow and become more truly themselves:

- Humanistic psychology enshrines a belief that if you get the environment right and allow a human being to develop as they truly are, everything else will fall into place.
- Cognitive behavioural psychology sees behaviour as a function of stimulus and response. If we can map our thoughts and feelings and the connections between them as well as between them and the environment, we shall be better able to function.
- The psychoanalytic schools see human beings as driven by unconscious memories and desires. The better we can get in touch with these, the freer we will be to live our lives fully.

There is also a significant rise in therapies that combine psychological help with mindfulness techniques taken from meditation traditions. These train people to place themselves in a frame of mind where they can allow thoughts and feelings to come and go without being overwhelmed by them and this, too, is a rich and promising field.

All these psychological approaches – including mindfulness – have echoes and counterparts in the Christian tradition. It may not always be helpful to try to draw the analogies too closely, but psychology as we understand it today is nothing new: what is new in the last 150 years is the systematization of it in a secular form.

Whatever their theoretical basis, the psychological therapies differ significantly from the practice of pastoral care. They tend to be built around firm boundaries, reliability of time and space, and privacy, all of which are intended to nurture a relationship well enough contained to allow risks to be taken and thoughts and feelings to emerge and be shared – and even transformed. Such firm structures are usually an unheard-of luxury in pastoral care, which may take place on the street, in a youth club or on a crowded hospital ward, and pastoral supervisors need to be aware that however secure the supervision environment, the working environment may be something else altogether.

Therapy or counselling and pastoral care, then, inhabit two quite different traditions, and pastoral supervision is a place where these impact on each other. Supervisor and supervisee may have quite different understandings of what to expect from an encounter and this can raise difficult questions to which there are no obvious answers. For example, it is often argued by pastoral carers that doing something practical is more use than probing people's feelings. Supervisors, on the other hand, may feel that the supervisee has failed to enter into the feelings being expressed – and that this may be a self-protective move.

For example, Jill offered pastoral listening in a church setting. A young man whose girlfriend had been killed in an accident said to her, 'People say God is suffering with me. And I think, "Thanks a lot, God. How about doing something a bit more constructive?"' Eager to help, Jill offered him some tapes on suffering, which she herself had found useful at a difficult time. As Jill's supervisor, how would you react? You might say she had missed a valuable opportunity to explore the man's anger and other feelings that lay behind that protest. Or you might agree that she was meeting him on common ground by offering something that had helped her – acknowledging that she too had needed help at a difficult time. Was she coming alongside, or was she putting up a barrier, defending herself against his pain?

Just what the supervisor's responsibilities are in this situation will vary depending on the context. If Jill were seeking to act as a counsellor, her intervention should certainly be challenged. But if she is simply there to come alongside people and is not trained to handle strong feeling, perhaps she should simply be supported in what she is doing. What is Jill's implicit contract with the bereaved man? How much time do they have? Given the way she responded, does Jill in any case need to be encouraged to explore her own feelings about bereavement and/or her own anger with God? In a situation like this, can supervisor and supervisee learn from each other about how we operate in different contexts?

These kinds of questions highlight something of the culture clash that can be experienced when we apply supervision as understood in the world of therapy and counselling to the complex field of pastoral care.

In bridging the gap, perhaps room can be found for mutual respect between theology and psychology by talking about the theological basis of pastoral supervision in a way that makes room for psychological insight. Our theological starting point for this is the phrase from Ephesians: being 'rooted and grounded in love' (Eph. 3.17). Using this idea, we can perhaps evolve a theological framework for pastoral supervision that is trinitarian in nature, representing in its practice the three Persons of the Trinity by being:

- relational – calling us into being by love, and creating community;
- incarnational – bringing psychological realism and rigour to pastoral contexts;
- open to the movement of the Spirit.

Rooted and grounded in love

Being rooted and being grounded are both essential to individuals engaged in spiritual and/or psychological growth, as well as to communities attempting to grow together. Paul's prayer in the letter to the Ephesians is that being rooted and grounded in love – that is, planted in and built on love – Christ will live in their hearts through faith so that they will have the strength to grasp 'breadth and length, height and depth' (Eph. 3.17–18): in other words, to know the full extent God's involvement in the world.

As we can see from this picture, what we see of a plant is only a tiny part of what enables it to grow:

- Roots come up from below and grow down from above. To be *rooted* is to be able go down deep into the earth, to draw nourishment from the fertile darkness.
- To be *grounded* is to have a firm base from which to reach upwards and outwards into the light and air. We are programmed, if you like, to grow, to seek, to expand, and a good foundation enables us to do that.

'I am the vine and you are the branches', says Jesus in his long discourse just before the Passion. 'Those who abide in me and I in them bear much fruit' (John 15.1). The vine is rooted in the good earth of love and the branches reach out to bear fruit because they are grounded in the vine which is Christ; the small shoots open to and seek the Spirit. Every one of them is interdependent, and yet each is living a life that is their own.

To be rooted and grounded in love is to know the invisible, transcendent world as well as the everyday material world. It is to know the Christ who lived among us in history as well as the universal, cosmic Christ, the universal Logos who is the deep structure of everything that is. It is through Christ the Logos that roots and seeds grow into the plants that they are meant to be, and it is through Christ, the Logos, that we too grow, seeking out our true nature. It is in this way, Paul tells the Ephesians, that they will be fellow citizens and part of God's household (Eph. 2.19). For us, too, in order to engage fruitfully in pastoral supervision we need some understanding of how and where we belong in that household.

Pastoral supervision is relational

We can think of the creative power of the Father as the source of all being that brings all things into being through love, pouring itself out over the world just as a waterfall pours itself out and spreads in all directions when it reaches the valley. In this context 'relational' means much more than a relationship between two human beings or between a person and God. It involves the relationship of all of us to each other and to God – and every other person's relationship to God as well. This is inescapable, but easily forgotten.

Peter was a pastoral counsellor who spent many hours each week listening to people in his church community who were in distress. He also prayed for them at home and this helped to sustain him in his work. One day, however, he was praying for the people he worked with when he realized that he was plain bored – and this made him feel guilty and lost. He brought this to supervision and in talking about it he saw that his clients and their problems had taken over from what had been a conversation between him and God. Far from being sustained, he felt pulled in

different directions. Either he drew closer to God and forgot the
people he cared for, or he drew closer to them, and felt cut off
from God, as in Figure 1:

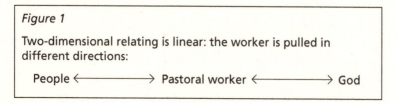

Figure 1

Two-dimensional relating is linear: the worker is pulled in
different directions:

People ⟵⟶ Pastoral worker ⟵⟶ God

'What about your clients', asked his supervisor, 'do they have any
connection with God?' Peter thought for a moment and then said,
'Yes'. After a further short silence he said that he needed to stand
back a bit, to allow the prayer space to open out. If he could
remember that God loved each of these people, he could spend
less time brooding on their difficulties. God could take care of
his own relationships with them, and he, Peter, would be free
to relate to them at a human level as well as to enter into his
own relationship with God. The space in which he prayed could
become three-dimensional as in Figure 2.

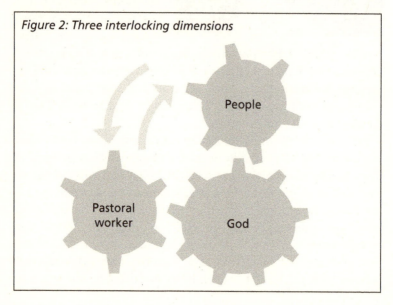

Figure 2: Three interlocking dimensions

In this model, whatever goes on between the pastoral worker and the people in her or his care takes place in the context of both the worker and each and every one of those people being rooted and grounded in God's love. The same applies to the supervision relationship. The supervisee's work is contained in the encounter between supervisor and supervisee, but every party to that – supervisor, supervisee and each of the people concerned – has an individual as well as a communal relationship with God, everyone concerned being a member of God's household.

It is when we move into this territory – the communal nature of our being rooted and grounded in love – that it can become difficult to talk about it in a way that is psychologically rigorous. The insights of counselling psychology speak far more easily to spirituality as an individual journey than to religion as a communal enterprise (what we might call the 'household' aspect of spirituality). Not only do many religious institutions demonize psychology, but psychologists are rightly critical of many of the ways in which religious institutions often behave. It is not surprising, then, that we can find ourselves losing sight of the value of community in religious experience.

For example, in his chapter on the spirituality of supervision in *Integrative Approaches to Supervision*, Michael Carroll draws on Sam Keen's distinctions between spirituality and religion:[1]

- One is about answers, the other about questions.
- One is about obedience, the other about openness, waiting and trust.
- One is about repetition, the other about inventing, creating.
- One is about sacred places and objects, the other is about sacred people.
- One is about ascending, the other about descending.
- One is based on other worlds, the other finds the sacred in life and work.
- One is institutional and corporate, the other is individual and communal.

---

1 M. Carroll, M. and M. Tholstrup (eds), 2001, *Integrative Approaches to Supervision*, London and Philadelphia: Jessica Kingsley, chapter 6.

- One is about rising above it all, the other is about being immersed in it.

Most people with some experience of church life will have sympathy with what Sam Keen has to say about what happens to religious institutions. His basic argument is that all human beings share a capacity for awe and wonder, and this is the doorway through which we will find compassion and connection. This is certainly the case, but the implication of the above list is that those things Keen ascribes to religion – obedience, repetition, sacred places and so on – are less valuable than those ascribed to spirituality, whereas in fact they are essential building blocks of God's household: of whatever community, that is, that sustains us in our faith.

Carroll goes on to use Keen's distinctions to differentiate between what he calls 'religious' and 'spiritual' supervision:

> Supervision in the religious mode has all the answers, is well mapped, has calls for obedience and is about sacred ways. Supervision that is spiritual is the opposite. It goes to search, to be with, to think through, to find pathways that last for a while, and then these pathways are no more.[2]

This is an inspiring model: it offers flexibility and freedom not to know the answers. These are things that supervisors and supervisees in pastoral work often find it hard to allow themselves and each other. It also, however, disregards the fact that all those aspects called 'spiritual' – the liberating aspects – belong in our religious traditions, even if they are not always highly visible in religious organizations. Healthy religion has spirituality at its heart, and if we jettison religion relying only on spirituality, we lose some valuable aspects of supervision – including being well mapped, having at least some answers, calling for obedience (in the sense that we all need to be obedient to the necessities of our situation) and, indeed, sacred ways.

---

2 Carroll and Tholstrup (eds), *Integrative Approaches to Supervision*, p. 80.

One way of thinking about what is missing is to think of the four functions defined by Jung in his theory of personality – his typology (which many pastoral carers encounter through the Myers-Briggs Type Indicator). According to Jung, each of us has four functions, or ways of perceiving and processing the world. These are in pairs of opposites, each of which is essential to the healthy functioning of the other:

- Intuition – Sensation
- Feeling – Thinking

Any one of us has and uses all four ways of dealing with the world, but one of each pair will be more conscious and highly developed.

Intuition and sensation are different ways of perceiving. Intuition gives us hunches, vision, the big picture: people who are naturally intuitive need help in noticing detail and staying with what is. Having a strong sensation function means you are very aware of what you perceive with your senses: you read the small print, you measure things before you start a job and so on. People with a strong sensation function may need help in looking to the future and to the bigger picture.

Feeling and thinking are different ways of processing information. Someone with a strong feeling function will be generally good at evaluating their emotional reactions – and other people's – while someone with a strong thinking function has a good logical grasp of whatever is going on.[3]

When psychology critiques religion and veers off into spirituality, we often find ourselves immersed in intuition and feeling without the balancing functions of sensation and thinking. To supervise and be supervised (or indeed to do anything at all effectively) we need to pay some attention to all four functions, even though our natural tendencies and capabilities will tend to one side or the other. Intuition and feeling open us to a sense of the beyond and to emotional intelligence. Sensation and thinking are

---

3 See C. G. Jung, 1987, *Dictionary of Analytical Psychology*, London: Routledge.

needed to remind us of structure, and of what people actually believe and experience as part of faith communities.

Carroll is right, of course, to critique faith communities for being rigid, demanding too much obedience and even abusing their members (though the same things can, or course, also be said about psychological professional institutions). Sadly, criticisms of religion are based in reality and to be part of God's household is increasingly problematic for many believers today. Only recently a priest said to me that she had often encountered compassion, sharing, generosity, basic human kindness – but never in a church context. This is not a new phenomenon. Jesus himself clearly had difficulties with the mainstream religious behaviour of his day, and over the centuries his followers have seemed determined to re-create the very things he criticized.

People involved in pastoral care inevitably belong to different traditions and have different practices. While some will be priests or ministers, others may not take any active part in any church community, but the fact that they engage in this kind of work suggests that they are interested in relating what they believe to what they do, and wish to do this not simply as searching individuals.

Belonging actively to a church means being part of a particular community, and to find a community that is containing and nourishing and where you can share worship with others on a regular basis is a wonderful thing. For those who do not manage to find this but who nevertheless belong, in a deep sense, to a community of faith, it is important to be able to define ways in which it is still possible to identify themselves as members of God's household. It may be important to bear in mind that, even at its best, any church is only a tiny manifestation of what church is. We can see the whole of creation, as a revelation of God's creativity, as a church. This is what Sam Keen is getting at (though he would not use this language) when he talks about 'dwelling in the presence of the sacred'.[4]

For example, a man called Jack was dying of cancer during a particularly delicious spring season; two friends accompanied

---

4 See, for example, S. Keen, 2010, *In the Absence of God: Dwelling in the Presence of the Sacred*, New York: Harmony Books.

him and his wife in the sadness of his final months. The beauty of the spring was something they all shared: however great their sadness, that beauty made it worthwhile to be alive. Jack was a regular churchgoer, his wife less so, and the friends not at all. But for those few, intense weeks, the beauty of nature bound them together in a faith community.

There is, then, a sense in which the Church is already universal: it is a vast community in which we can begin to glimpse 'the height, the depth, the length and the breadth' of the love of Christ (Eph. 3.18). It is also a community in which psychological insight has grown and developed over time. That insight forms part of our spiritual journey, and has enabled us as individuals and communities to grow in love. To be truly rooted and grounded in love, however, we have to allow ourselves to be rigorous about and suspicious of love – or what we mean by love – *at the same time as* being alert to what is being revealed about its breadth and length, its height and depth. This has been the path of religious people from time immemorial.

A theological framework for pastoral supervision, then, takes very seriously our belonging at many levels. It involves many kinds of belonging: to a community or workplace or institution, to a psychological tradition, and to a faith tradition, however we might practise that. Bringing all the four psychological functions – intuition, sensation, thinking and feeling – can help us to define our own ways of belonging and our understanding of the communities and organizations to which we belong, and what they require of us. We may be at the centre or we may be at the edge, but even – or perhaps especially – at the edge, we can still experience ourselves as members of the household.

Pastoral supervision is incarnational

In the space inhabited by supervisor and supervisee we find the people the supervisee works with, the people who have contributed to the experience of both, the institutions and communities to whom they belong, and countless different experiences of God.

These are our sources of understanding. How do we give them form?

In its incarnational mode pastoral supervision can make a bridge between psychology and theology. It brings insight into the way people actually are; it insists on rigour – and it is realistic. It knows there are limits to what can be done. Incarnation means giving form and substance to the love that lies behind the universe. The Incarnation of Christ is a particular instance of this, but the incarnation of love is something that is going on all the time.

Two great figures – one a theologian and one a psychologist – reached similar conclusions about this at very different times in human history. In the sixth century, while reflecting on the Incarnation of Christ, the theologian Maximus the Confessor wrote: 'God wishes always and everywhere to bring about the mystery of his embodiment.'[5] He was describing God's self-revelation in human beings and in the cosmos – and he emphasizes that this self-revelation is driven by God's own desire.

Some thirteen centuries later, C. G. Jung wrote, 'Ever since John the apocalyptician [the writer of Revelation] ... mankind has groaned under this burden: God wanted to become man, and still wants to.'[6] Here we have a bridge between our two disciplines: two great figures, who arrive independently at the same insight, Maximus by reflecting on the relationship between God and the world, Jung by going deep into the human psyche.

Here we also have an image of God as the love in which we are rooted, giving forth energy, expanding, desiring to embody himself in the created universe. Again, this is what Sam Keen is talking about when he refers to the sacredness of everything that is, and it is why people have what he calls primary experiences of the holy.

Another concept used by Sam Keen, which was also part of the world view of the early Church Fathers, is the idea of human beings as the microcosm of the macrocosm. Creation consists

---

5 Ambigua 7.
6 C. G. Jung, 1954, *Answer to Job*, London, Routledge, p. 153.

both of what we can see, feel and touch, and also of the unseen world of the spirit (the empathy that exists within a supervision encounter is part of this unseen world). As human beings we stand at the meeting point of these seen and unseen worlds, and mediate between them. In a sense, then, everything that is passes through us.

We could also say that the supervision encounter is itself a meeting point not only of the individuals themselves, and the people involved in the work that is brought into the session, but also all those things from which the supervisor draws authority and the supervisee draws trust: the supervision covenant, the requirements of the institution, the training and experience of supervisor and supervisee, the context in which the supervisee works. The nature of the supervisor's responsibility means he or she has to challenge as well as nurture and encourage.

For people working in a Christian context, a significant resource in this incarnational mode is the gospel itself, with its many stories that resonate with people's experience, and the liturgical cycle that grows out of these stories and becomes woven into people's lives at many different levels.

These stories can also give us courage. We are all familiar with the idea that Jesus was loving and compassionate, but it is important also to remember that his interventions are often robust, ironic or playful. Asked, for example, if people should pay their taxes, he does not answer directly but says, 'Show me a coin' and points to Caesar's head on it (Matt. 22.19). For many people the most shocking encounter in the Gospels – and the only one where Christ loses the argument – is with the Canaanite woman begging him to heal her daughter. He protests that he was sent to the lost children of the House of Israel, and she replies, 'True, Lord, but even dogs eat the crumbs that fall from their master's table' (Matt. 15.27). One thing we can learn from these encounters is that while of course we must affirm, nurture and encourage, in order to incarnate love, we must also not be afraid to challenge, to play, to trigger a spontaneous response.

Pastoral supervision is open to the Spirit

In the Incarnation of Christ the whole world becomes concentrated in a human person. Through the life, death and resurrection of that person transformation takes place, and the way is prepared for the coming of the Spirit. A new age is born. 'Unless I leave you,' Christ says to his disciples, 'the Comforter cannot come' (John 16.7). Supervisors, too, have to be willing to stand aside and make room for something creative and fresh to come from the encounter.

The psychological importance of firm ground from which we can go out and be creative is well known. Everyone needs to internalize enough basic trust to be able to act independently. Likewise, pastoral carers need to go out from the physical presence of the supervisor and be who they are in the outside world, carrying within them the nurture and self-knowledge they take away from the encounter.

In pastoral supervision a number of 'microcosms' become concentrated in a small space as supervisor and supervisee(s) bring their worlds into contact with each other. Potentially this contains huge energy, as when a river runs through the channel of a

millstream. Things can happen. Risks can be taken. What is stuck can be freed, what is shameful can be aired, what is joyful can be celebrated.

Earlier in this chapter, the outpouring love of the Father – the source of all being – was compared with a water source, a river that bubbles up and pours itself out into the landscape. If we think of that river channelled into a narrow millstream, we know that its energy becomes concentrated there, to drive the wheel of the mill.

Then, as it is released from the millstream, that energy is liberated and dissipates into the surrounding world. Though the water is no longer under our focus or under our control, it is still creative. We can perhaps think of the supervision encounter as a narrow channel or funnel through which experience passes, is given form and emerges in a new form. This is as true for the supervisor as it is for the supervisees.

This brings us to the third aspect of pastoral supervision in a theological framework. It is open to grace, to the movement of the Spirit: the Spirit of truth and of creativity.

The Spirit blows where it wills (John 3.8), and will not be tied down by our assumptions. It releases us into more effective practice:

- It gives us the courage to risk going beyond 'niceness'.
- It enables us to refrain from making rigid assumptions about shared faith and to respect differences.
- It helps us to accept that people are autonomous and can change, and that sometimes this seems to have nothing whatsoever to do with our interventions.

It is here, perhaps, that we find ourselves closest to Carroll's definition of supervision that is spiritual. Encouraged by the Spirit we can take risks. We can be prepared to search and find new pathways, aware that those pathways may nevertheless themselves change or even disappear.

A theological framework

These three aspects of supervision – relational, incarnational and open to the movement of the Spirit – can also express a community of faith, however loosely that faith may be defined. We can allow for our own and other people's creativity while remembering that we are members of God's household.

Within this theological framework, as shown in Figure 3, we can also allow the insights of psychology to speak as well as to sustain and guide us while being at the same time rooted and grounded in love:

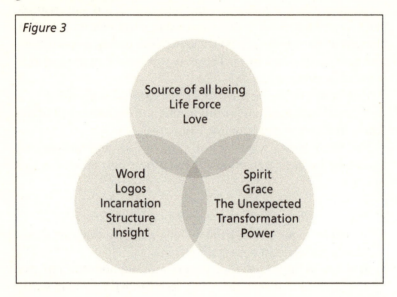

Figure 3

Source of all being
Life Force
Love

Word
Logos
Incarnation
Structure
Insight

Spirit
Grace
The Unexpected
Transformation
Power

This Trinitarian framework is not tied to any particular psychological approach, but perhaps it gives us a way to flesh out our sense of the sacred alongside our insights into human nature. As with the water going through the millstream, we can subject these insights to a rigorous and energizing process, to emerge in a new form. Some questions that might offer a starting point are:

- What is my faith community? Is it a community with which I worship or is it some other, looser network of friends, colleagues, the people I work with?
- What is my psychological community: the understanding of human beings that makes sense to me, and helps me understand what is going on in an encounter?
- Am I sufficiently rooted in these not to be threatened by other people's beliefs and approaches being different from my own?
- Am I sufficiently grounded in them to expand, to seek what is new, to grow?

These questions may help to put the framework into practice. Anyone's answers may – and almost certainly will – change and develop over time, and those answers may point in new directions, reflecting the ongoing energy of the outpouring of the Father, the continuing incarnational presence of the Son and the inspiration of the Spirit.

Risking the Embodied Self: A Theology of Presence in Pastoral Supervision

EWAN KELLY

This chapter explores the use of the reflexive self within pastoral supervision. Emphasis is placed not only on reflection on practice but also on reflecting in practice. Transformative practice arises from attending to the emotional, spiritual, physical/sensual, imaginative and sexual aspects of our humanity. Such practical wisdom embraces rather than shuns risk and reconnects the supervisee with the values and beliefs at the core of their professional identity.

Introduction

> ...what is actual is actual only for one time
> And only for one place.
> T. S. Eliot[1]

The reflexive self is a key therapeutic resource in the provision of spiritual and pastoral care. Hertz helpfully describes reflexivity as 'an ongoing conversation about experience while simultaneously living in the moment'.[2] Similarly, within the context of pastoral

---

1 T. S. Eliot, 1974, 'Ash Wednesday', *Collected Poems 1909–1962*, London: Faber & Faber, p. 85.

2 R. Hertz, 1997, 'Introduction: Reflexivity and Voice', in *Reflexivity and Voice*, Thousand Oaks, CA: Sage, pp. vii–xviii, viii.

supervision knowledge of self, gleaned from reflection on past experience and utilization of such awareness in the here and now, is central to the transformative learning opportunity co-created by supervisor and supervisee. In supervisory practice, as in pastoral practice, there may be a temptation to focus on the application of learnt techniques and theory rather than utilize the embodied self, informed by practical wisdom, to respond in the reality of supervisory moments. Hiding behind acquired knowledge and theoretical expertise can be a protective means to minimize exposure to the messiness and angst of others' experience in practice. Perhaps more significantly, it may reveal unwillingness on the supervisor's part to be open to, and honest about, personal fears and anxiety relating to, for example, dealing with uncertainty and helplessness.

Supervision marries attention to what supervisors and supervisees are aware of prior to meeting – that is, what has been learnt by reflection *on* practice – to the role of self-knowledge being utilized discerningly in the actuality of a one-off time and place. To perform the art of pastoral supervision is to embody reflection *in* practice. To do so involves listening intently to the senses – listening to and hearing what the senses (including the whole body itself), head, heart and gut are communicating in the present moment of supervision. More than that, it is then being intentionally willing to risk responding and acting on such intuitive information with *phronesis* or practical wisdom.[3] In doing so both the supervisee and supervisor will have greater opportunity to deepen learning, and transform future practice and understanding of self (including the values and beliefs that shape personal and professional identity) in practice. Doing theology together in a pastoral supervisory context is therefore not only a cognitive exercise but one that involves the whole of ourselves – the emotional, spiritual, physical/sensual, imaginative and sexual aspects of our humanity.

---

3 *Phronesis* being the creative and discerning use of knowledge (including awareness of self) in the moment acquired through ongoing reflective practice and engagement with a relevant evidence base informing current practice.

Within a supervisory context a supervisee is invited to risk being vulnerable – to share stories of their practice and reflect on what may inform and shape it, in order that the relationship between vocational and personal identity may be explored. There is a need for the supervisee to be motivated to risk engaging with the uncomfortable and what may rise up from his unconscious. In other words, to be open to the unexpected, and perhaps unwanted, and to be prepared to be confronted with the hitherto half-known or unrecognized parts of himself, including his motivations and fantasies regarding ministry. There is an intentionality required by the supervisee to be prepared to explore and wrestle with that which may emerge from a supervisory relationship which influences his practice, his way of being and relating in a pastoral role. Graham, Walton and Ward (also quoting Schön) put it this way – 'They (professionals) need to be proactive learners and risk-takers. Practitioners must "move into the centre of the learning situation, into the centre of their own doubts".'[4] Similarly, the supervisor is also called to risk in order that a relationship of 'shared vulnerability'[5] may be developed where the emphasis is not on telling the 'right story', making the 'correct' discoveries or responding 'accurately'. It is co-constructing a relationship and shared space of trust, playfulness and provisionality where all persons involved are willing and feel able to risk being open to new learning and potential transformation. The supervisor has responsibility for boundarying and holding the space utilizing her authority discerningly to do so, yet, paradoxically if she does not risk making intentional use of her embodied self and her intuitional responses to the narrative of the other(s), then little meaningful sharing or learning will occur. What is significant in such a supervisory context is the process of learning (verb), including supervisory modelling of informed risk-taking and taking a lead in enabling

---

4 E. Graham, H. Walton and F. Ward, 2005, *Theological Reflection: Methods*, London: SCM Press, p. 4; D. Schön, 1983, *The Reflective Practitioner: How Professionals Think in Action*, New York: Basic Books, p. 83.

5 M. Browne, 2013, 'Developing Shame Resilience through Pastoral Supervision', *Reflective Practice: Formation and Supervision in Ministry* 33, p. 66.

'shared vulnerability' in the supervisory space, not just the product or outcome that is the learning (noun) or transformation.[6]

What do we risk?

Rejection

Pastoral supervision is an embodied and performative art. Practising that art with *phronesis* involves investment of the whole self (or as much as can be offered at a particular time) in attentiveness to the other(s), to the supervisor's own internal world and her embodiment of that world and what happens between all involved. It is a draining and exacting art form, an example of what American pastoral theologian Pamela Cooper-White calls 'intersubjectivity', 'an ongoing dance of mutual influence – an "intersubjective" relationship both conscious and unconscious' between supervisor and supervisee(s).[7] It means risking acting on hunches and bodily sensations at the discerned appropriate moment in response to the verbal or enacted narrative shared or the underlying meaning glimpsed. It is about risking an intervention that may be challenging or stretching not just affirming. Within such a relational paradigm pastoral supervision is an interpretative and provisional dance, the difference between supervisee and supervisor being not in the level of significance of their interpretation or depth of meaning of their offering but in their roles and responsibilities. Cooper-White emphasizes this further:

> In the relational paradigm, responsibility shifts from issues of ownership, control and technique to something that is perhaps even more ethically demanding: commitment to authenticity,

---

6 T. Fenwick, 2010, 'Workplace "Learning" and Adult Education: Messy Objects, Blurry Maps and Making Difference', *European Journal for Research on the Education and Learning of Adults* 1:1–2, pp. 79–95.

7 Cooper-White writes of 'intersubjectivity' within the context of pastoral counselling but her concept also has application as outlined here within supervisory relationships. P. Cooper-White, 2004, *Shared Wisdom: Use of Self in Pastoral Care and Counselling*, Minneapolis: Fortress Press, p. 57.

integrity, faithfulness to focussing on the growth and well-being of the one seeking help, and a new form of self-commitment to self-examination – especially because one's own subjectivities have come to be understood in the relational model as simply one point of observation of the entire intersubjective field that lies, continually in flux, between both participants in the field.[8]

To play safe and practise supervision competently by merely applying learnt techniques and theoretical knowledge without trusting and maximizing the resources of the reflexive self may be to lessen risk and reduce anxieties and fears about 'getting things wrong', being disliked or rejected by supervisees for offering interpretations or creative interjections that are experienced as too uncomfortable or perceived as being mistaken. However, to supervise in this way is to limit the opportunity for learning and possibilities for transformation for all involved. In learning to trust instincts and be open and attentive to 'gut feelings' (or in theological terms discerning the promptings of the Spirit within and around self and between self and others) is to risk exploring new possibilities, landscapes and depths. This is supervision with courage and integrity. It is to create supervisory spaces which 'respond to the invitation of grace'.[9]

Misuse of power

One aspect of the reflexive use of the embodied self in supervision which requires close attention by the supervisor (and if sufficiently aware also by the supervisee) to optimize a shared learning experience is use of power. This includes authority and status which the supervisor possesses through accumulation of theoretical knowledge and that acquired through the development of professional wisdom in comparison to that of her supervisees. In addition, there may also be the subjective status and power projected on to a

8 Cooper-White, *Shared Wisdom*, p. 60.

9 T. O'Connor, 1998, *Clinical Pastoral Supervision and the Theology of Charles Gerkin*, Waterloo, Ontario: Wilfred Laurier University Press, p. 5.

supervisor informed by supervisees' relationships with significant 'authority figures' in their pasts. How a supervisor utilizes such power for good or ill is heavily dependent on reflexivity, integrity and compassion.[10] To enter a supervisory relationship is to risk the inadvertent or even advertent misuse of power. Key questions around the issue of power in supervisory relationships are worth pondering. For example, how much power can a supervisor give away in any one moment of supervision to empower another, yet still maintain responsibility for holding the boundaries and containing the relationship/group? Wise and discerning use of power, both giving it away and/or firmly holding on to it, can deepen engagement or squash it, for one or all involved in a supervisory moment. Such *phronetic* use of power resonates with themes in feminist pastoral theology, which involves intentional risking and a desire to promote fulfilment and well-being in others (and thus enhancing meaning and purpose for a supervisor):

> Women find the exercise of power more satisfying if it simultaneously enhances the lives of others. Roles and careers traditionally assigned to women presuppose such attention to developing and nurturing others gifts: motherhood, teaching, nursing. Enabling others is a central goal of women in ministry. Yet this is real power.[11]

Our sexual selves

Anglican priest and spiritual writer Jim Cotter writes, 'my sexuality pervades and permeates my unique being: I sense it as inextricably bound up with my identity as a person'.[12] Those involved

---

10 This is not to say supervisees are not without power also. For example, feelings of countertransference within a supervisor will be provoked in supervisory relationships which also may be used unconsciously or consciously by supervisees to influence the relationship.

11 K. Fischer, 1989, *Women at the Well: Feminist Perspectives on Spiritual Direction*, London: SPCK, p. 142, cited by Graham et al., *Theological Reflection: Methods*, p. 184.

12 J. Cotter, 1988, *Pleasure, Pain and Passion: Some Perspectives on Sexuality and Spirituality*, Sheffield: Cairns Publications, p. 5.

in pastoral supervision are sexual beings. That is to say who we are and how we understand and feel about ourselves as embodied men and women impacts on how any of us, as supervisor or supervisee, relates to others and ourselves in a pastoral supervisory space. 'As sexual beings all our relationships have a sexual dimension. We relate through our bodies and we relate through our gender.'[13] How we communicate ourselves, our ideas, our feelings, our beliefs and our values is done through our physicality as much as by our words or our silence. More than that, it is not just what we do with our bodies that communicates much – our gestures, our presence or absence and our touch – but how we do so that is significant. What we intentionally communicate with our bodies or indeed intuitively enact in supervisory spaces requires us to risk – to dare to use our bodies in sensual, creative and affirming ways. If we take touch as an example of such enactment – touch intended to affirm, to convey solidarity or to console – then indeed it is to risk. Touching another, for example, is to risk misinterpretation of sexual attraction or to prematurely subdue expression of another's distress and upset. Lack of reflexivity and discernment regarding whether to touch, where and when may lead to a mis-use of power and an infantilization or manipulation of a supervisee to meet a supervisor's own need and gratification. However, appropriate timely touch may convey compassion and encouragement, deepening trust and enabling fuller honest engagement. Intentional use of the embodied reflexive self as a sexual being is to risk hurting or being hurt or rejected, to risk getting it wrong, but not to do so is to limit use of self as a resource for meaningful pastoral supervision.[14]

---

13 M. Shanahan, 1997, 'Celibacy: A Subversive Proclamation of Christian Freedom or Sexual Repression', in K. Galloway (ed.), *Dreaming of Eden: Reflections on Christianity and Sexuality*, Glasgow: Wild Goose Publications, p. 90.

14 For fuller exploration of the use of touch and the sexual self in caring and creative relationships, not necessarily supervisory ones, see K. Litchfield, 2006, *Tend My Flock: Sustaining Good Pastoral Care*, Norwich: Canterbury Press; M. Lyall, 1997, 'The Pastoral Counselling Relationship: A Touching Place?', *Contact Pastoral Monograph* 7, Edinburgh: Contact Pastoral Trust.

Our vulnerable selves – towards a theology embracing risk

'Keep looking. Keep looking, even when there's not much to see. That way your eye learns what's common, so that when the uncommon appears your eye will tell you.'[15]

Attentiveness, according to Scots poet Kathleen Jamie, is the key to observing nature and experiencing numinous moments where new discoveries, connections and understandings are made. Reflecting on practice, the telling and enacting, listening to and observing stories of pastoral relationships is not always a dynamic and energizing process. It involves sifting through the ordinary, the oft experienced and the recollected. It involves waiting and remaining attentive for the cross-grain, the different, the pearl of great price to emerge in the actuality of a particular time and place. It risks staying with the mundane, even the boring, and being familiar with their patterns so that the treasure which points to possible transformation and glimpses of transcendence may be intuited and mined for.[16]

Such waiting also means being open to times of uncertainty when we genuinely don't know what will emerge in the negotiated supervisory space. It means risking a lack of control of what may come out of the depths of self or inter-relating while being in a supervisory relationship. Making the self vulnerable and open in such a way is an active choice not a passive happening.[17] Seamus Heaney in his address when being awarded the Nobel Prize for poetry said, 'What "always will be to poetry's credit" is "the power to persuade that vulnerable part of our consciousness of its rightness in spite of all the evidence of wrongness all around it."'[18] This is an important task of the pastoral supervisor. Yet, American pastoral theologian Herb Anderson is also right to ask: how

---

15 K. Jamie, 2012, *Sightlines*, London: Sort of Books, p. 82.

16 See S. Waters, 2012, 'Getting More than You Paid For: The Parable of the Treasure and the Pearl as the Experience of Transformation', *Pastoral Psychology* 61:4, pp. 423–34.

17 V. Herrick, 1997, 'Limits of Vulnerability', Grove Pastoral Series 71, Cambridge: Grove.

18 Cited by C. Higgins and H. McDonald, 2013, 'Seamus Heaney's Death Leaves a Breach in Language Itself', *Guardian*, 31 August 2013, p. 3.

much awareness of vulnerability can we endure? To repeatedly, intentionally and reflexively enter the unknown of supervisory relationships is to be aware of exposure to vulnerability and to seek to live with it 'without being overwhelmed by it'.[19] In engaging with issues of vocation, fulfilment in work and the impact of ministry on personal beliefs and motivations, both supervisor and supervisees are confronted with the 'vulnerable part of our consciousness' including issues of core meaning and purpose and faith in life.

Perhaps one of the most profound risks faced by participating in pastoral supervision is the possible discovery, or rather ownership of the previously un-named feeling of 'an underlying despair of what should be most certain in my life',[20] that life in the present has little meaning or depth; that what was once vocational now brings little joy and is devoid of an engaged faith; that what we currently embody is not so much a life with purpose but a habituated existence. Melbourne poet Aileen Kelly in 'The Windows' depicts how such loss of direction, purpose and fulfilment can potentially creep up on us as well as be forced upon us by significant losses and transitions. She depicts the kind of state that leads to accidie and melancholia and struggles with a sense of self where a practitioner's very identity, contribution and worth are called into question.

Somehow it slips by him every night.
His wife, snug in her kitchen window-niche,
Watches the birds scatter and fold to silence.
His hand moves to press his desk lamp switch
Without awareness of the changing light.
She enters sometime soon without disturbance,
Places a glass of sherry to his reach,
Quietly steps round to draw his curtains.

19 H. Anderson, 2013, 'Head and Heart: Renewing Spirituality for Ministry Preparation', in *Reflective Practice: Formation and Supervision in Ministry* 33, p. 91.
20 R. S. Thomas, 1993, 'Who?', *Collected Poems 1945–1990*, London: Phoenix Giants, p. 177.

Somewhere there's an evening when she'll find
His life-habit empty in the usual place
In the unusual absence of the lamp's pool;

Or when, quite late, his gut will pinch his mind
to register they haven't had a meal
and the naked windows shock him with his own face.[21]

Overwork, unclear role identity, poor boundary keeping, the constancy of the demand of parishioners, patients or institutions, dealing with perceived failures and limitations and many other potential drains on those in ministry may lead to exhaustion and frustration. Ongoing immersion in other peoples' pain and suffering, regular exposure to the conflicts and frustrations of working in large organizations and systems, wrestling with issues of theodicy and the presence, even the very existence, of God can lead to more than a healthy doubting (potentially for supervisor or supervisee). It can lead to despair and utter disbelief leaving not only a gap in what underpins our practice but shaking the very foundations of what may give meaning and purpose to our livelihood and our daily living. Such spiritual questioning cannot be overcome by mere reason. As R. S. Thomas notes: 'someone must have thought of putting me here: It wasn't I that did it.'[22]

For those who are repeatedly exposed to the deep bruises, tensions, conflicts and loss in human life (as practitioner or supervisor) who can avoid at times calling into question what others and perhaps ourselves consider should be most certain in our lives? It is a healthy and normal response but it is invariably a hard and painful experience. It is to take a risk and for those in ministry (as pastors or supervisors), it is an intentional one – a choice to make ourselves vulnerable to such potential wounding and the inevitable subsequent inner questioning and searching. Yet, such risking is to be open to the possible development of a conjunctive

---

21 A. Kelly, 2006, *The Passion Paintings (Poems 1983–2006)*, Elwood, Victoria: John Leonard Press, p. 12. Used with permission.
22 Thomas, *Collected Poems 1945–1990*, p. 177.

faith,[23] that is, a faith that makes room for the contradictory, the relative and 'the recognition of the multifaceted nature of truth',[24] thus welcoming the need for imaginative, reflexive and creative theological inquiry.

On a recent visit to Uluru, in central Australia, I was fascinated to read the notice at the bottom of the rock encouraging us not to climb that sacred place in order to conquer it but to walk round it and connect with it. So it is with the anxieties and fears that arise within us before, or are noticed during or after particular supervisory sessions. The task for the reflexive supervisee or supervisor in this regard is not to conquer or overcome inner disquiet or niggling doubts, but to connect with them and wonder about them, exploring more fully what they are revealing. In this way a heightened understanding of the thoughts and feelings awakened within by exposure to others' stories in and about ministry may lead to a deepened understanding of self, other and the Other.

Doing theological reflection within pastoral supervision in such a manner is to develop an unsystematic theology – a theology of fragments. Scots practical theologian Duncan Forrester unpacks this concept further:

> Theological fragments, as I understand them, arise from, and relate to, specific situations, problems, contexts, issues and communities. But often insights from one specific situation are found to be of more general relevance. A theology of fragments hopes to contribute to throwing some light on what is going on, and challenging to constructive and faithful practice today.[25]

A theology of fragments involves honest reflection on the reality of human experience and pastoral practice. It is a theology that leaves room to say I don't know, that embraces paradox and allows space for doubts and questions and takes seriously

---

23 J. Fowler, 1996, *Faithful Change: The Personal and Public Challenges of Postmodern Life*, Nashville: Abingdon.

24 Lyall, 'Pastoral Counselling Relationship', p. 114.

25 D. Forrester, 2005, *Theological Fragments: Explorations in Unsystematic Theology*, London: T. & T. Clark, p. ix.

engagement with living human documents and systems and their socio-political contexts as well as sacred written texts to shape its formation and ongoing reformation. It is a theology that is based on connection and vulnerability, not power that is used to systematize, subdue and conquer. This is an approach to theology that embraces risk and reflexivity – having courage to risk being moved, challenged and changed in our attitudes towards, and our understanding of, ourselves in our vocational role in response to what is noticed and wondered about in supervisory moments.

Jean Vanier, the French Canadian philosopher and founder of the L'Arche community – a network of worldwide small communities where those with developmental disabilities live and share life with those who seek to assist them – writes:

> On the whole I can live quite peacefully today even though I know there is always anguish inside somewhere to be worked at. I am not good at dropping my barriers but I do the best I can. Our humanity is so beautiful but it needs to be transformed. We are called to live life everyday but also be open to the events, the encounter or meeting that can be transformative and that gives me a sense of the resurrection that is possible for us.[26]

Concluding thoughts – a theological underpinning

An approach to pastoral supervision that intentionally seeks to make best use of the reflexive embodied self in order to create opportunities for personal and professional growth requires a gentleness or tenderness of attitude towards self and the other(s) involved. Grace is something that is not just sought in supervisory spaces but is also required to be intentionally brought – a graciousness for all participants including self. God not only loves us (1 John 4.10) but calls us to love our neighbours as ourselves (Matt. 22.39). Part of that love is to display forgiveness of, and

---

26 J. Vanier, 2008, *Essential Writings*, London: Darton, Longman & Todd, p. 50.

gentleness with, self and others in supervisory relationships. In risking self through sharing stories, feelings, intuited hunches and discerned moments to intervene, even in a co-created safe space, there is opportunity to be hurt and to wound. Being secure in the fact that we are loved unconditionally by God not for what we do, say or achieve but for who we are is a significant requirement to enable risking honest sharing and reflection in pastoral supervision. In order to intentionally utilize the embodied reflexive self as the primary resource to facilitate the promotion of 'shared vulnerability' and real possibilities of learning and transformation within supervision, participants need to realize how lovable and loved by God each one is. The value to God of supervisor and supervisee does not depend on degrees of insight, ability to be open or appropriateness of sharing or intervention. If this is the theological basis for pastoral supervision, then grace truly may be responded to, meaning may be uncovered and fulfilment (re)found.

4

Can I Mean What I Say?
Thoughts on Language in
Pastoral Supervision[1]

CHARLES HAMPTON

'I would give anything to be more like him. I wish you would make me.' He did not say this in what might be called 'a particular manner'; perhaps he himself could not have said exactly what he meant by it. At that moment he had a curious feeling that he could say anything to her.

F. M. Mayor, The Rector's Daughter[2]

Truth lies not only in incidents but in hopes and needs.

Rebecca Solnit, A Field Guide to Getting Lost[3]

Introduction

In a graduation-day speech, the writer David Foster Wallace told the following story: There are these two young fish swimming along, and they happen to meet an older fish swimming the other way, who nods at them and says, 'Morning, boys. How's the water?' And the two young fish swim on for a bit, and then

---

1 The title is a borrowing from Stanley Cavell, 1969, *Must We Mean What We Say?*, New York: Scribner's. Angela is not the real name of the supervisee described in this chapter. She has given permission to use her story, and I am grateful to her for help in writing this. Related names have also been changed. Thanks also go to Neil Armstrong, Richard Gipps, Christine Miller and Jessica Rose for their constructive comments.

2 F. M. Mayor, 1973, *The Rector's Daughter*, Harmondsworth: Penguin.

3 R. Solnit, 2006, *A Field Guide to Getting Lost*, Edinburgh: Canongate.

eventually one of them looks over at the other and goes, 'What the ... is water?'[4]

Language can be compared to water. It is the medium of analytical thought, communication and much intentional action. Because vocabulary and grammar are in constant use, and because personal identity is bound up in our choice of how we express ourselves, it is not easy to stop and consider our relationship with speech and writing. It can even feel intrusive, as if our chosen nature is being criticized. But we should pay attention to it because, like water, it can become polluted, murky and sluggish. Like water, words can suffer drought and flood. Like water, language can be put to impersonal operational use, or it can assuage intimate need and desire.

In the particular case of pastoral supervision, language plays a role of exceptional importance, even if not all supervision chooses to emphasize it. Pastoral supervision has many roots in the 'Talking Cure', which at best can be a force for social peace and justice. In supervision, language can be purified of ignorance and malpractice and the effects of accident may be remedied. What can be more important than to ponder the way we speak to one another in our practice?

Two kinds of language

This chapter will focus on two contrasting kinds of language, using an incident brought to supervision by a clinical nurse specialist in palliative care. As a healthcare professional, Angela uses both of these kinds of language in the course of a normal working day. The first, which I will simply call Type A, believes in its own objectivity. The understanding that words always gain their meaning by referring to things is accepted without question. In Type A language, vocabulary draws upon a history of evolving meaning that settles contested interpretations in favour of a single relevant understanding. Angela makes use of this language in describing clinical symptoms to her colleagues. While exercising

---

4 D. Foster Wallace, 2009, *This is Water*, New York: Little, Brown and Co., p. 3.

necessary caution regarding the complexity of those symptoms, her words establish communication rapidly and efficiently. On this basis, decisions are made in order to relieve pain and manage medical conditions.

The other approach to language, which I will call Type B, sees its relation to the world as more problematic. It understands that grammar and vocabulary are public property, evolving over time, and that an individual must grapple with these in choosing how to express her personal thoughts and emotions. Angela uses this language in her pastoral role, when talking with dying patients and their relatives about the immediate future. There is a great deal for them to come to terms with, which naturally puts articulate speech under stress. It is language employed in the context of ultimate concerns, in which, as Murray Cox has put it, each of us 'is endeavouring to negotiate self-acceptance'.[5] Let us inquire a little further into its basis.

In *How (Not) to Speak of God* Peter Rollins has reminded us that 'Christian faith is born in the aftermath of God'.[6] To arrive late on the scene is also a feature of every human life. The idea that God (or indeed our parents) existed before we did can be hard to bear – a strange notion, but one borne out by experiences of irrational resentment. Language too, of course, pre-dates us, and learning to speak, read and write is an early exercise in submitting our will to the dictates of our culture. Coming late to history, our search for love must also accept compromise. Our mature expressions of gratitude and affection – what C. S. Lewis called 'gift-love'[7] – must endeavour to overcome the staleness of available vocabulary.

There is another obvious sense in which language demonstrates human limitations. As the story of the Babel Tower shows, we have to put up with the inconvenience of being separated from other cultures. The unity implicit in the idea of spirituality brings

---

5 M. Cox, 1988, *Structuring the Therapeutic Process*, London: Jessica Kingsley, p. 190.

6 P. Rollins, 2006, *How (Not) to Speak of God*, Brewster, MA: Paraclete Press, p. 1.

7 C. S. Lewis, 1960, *The Four Loves*, London: Fount.

us up against an equally inescapable diversity: *Dieu, Dio, Dia, Deus, Dios, Dievas, Gott, Gud, Bog, Theos, Drottinn, Dumnezeu, Jumaia, Isten, Elohim* are just a few of the European names for God. This perplexity in understanding one another, this constant need of translation, is not limited to encounters with foreigners. Within any language there exist not just dialects or specialized jargon, but rhetorical devices, teases, manipulations and seductions that can lead to misunderstanding.

Falling short does not, however, prevent us from reaching further. An approach faithful to the Jewish roots of Christianity acknowledges the inexpressible nature of God-given reality and works within the constraints of language in witnessing to it. Julia Kristeva has even suggested that putting a thought into words is in itself inseparable from an act of faith.[8] Metaphor can enact our desire as well as describing it. There is, moreover, a perception among certain poets that the world speaks back to us of its origins, as in Psalm 19:

> The heavens tell God's glory,
>   And His handiwork sky declares.
> Day to day breathes utterance
>   And night to night pronounces knowledge.
> There is no utterance and there are no words,
>   Their voice is never heard.
> Through all the earth their voice goes out,
>   To the world's edge, their words. (Psalm 19.1–2)

The editor of this translation, Robert Alter, comments on the seeming contradiction between the last two couplets:

> This is, of course, only the underlining of a moving paradox. The heavens speak, but it is a wordless language, what the great twentieth-century Hebrew poet H. N. Bialik would call 'the language of images'.[9]

---

8 J. Kristeva, 2009, *This Incredible Need to Believe*, New York: Columbia University Press, p. 3.

9 R. Alter, 2007, *The Book of Psalms*, New York: W. W. Norton, p. 60.

In characterizing two kinds of language in this way, I am not suggesting that they can claim the status of categories or exclude other possibilities: rather I am attempting to describe two instances of language-in-use within the caring professions. Figure 1 amplifies some of their characteristics.

Figure 1: Contrasting characteristics of two language-in-use types in the caring professions

Characteristics of Type A language-in-use	Characteristics of Type B language-in-use
Able to say what is (cataphatic)	Inclined to say what is not (apophatic)
Denoting	Enacting
Non-negotiable	Negotiable
Non-playful	Playful
Pointing out	Gesturing towards
Rule-bound	Rule-developing
Non-ironic	Ironic

The two kinds of language at odds with each other

The incident that Angela brought to supervision concerned a crisis in the relationship between these two types of language. Before going on to consider it, I will first explain how such a conflict might arise. The founder of linguistics, Ferdinand de Saussure, thought of language's task as being not to convey pre-existing meaning but rather to *effect* meaning by differentiating between things in the world.[10] It has always been important to name, for example, the foods that are safe to eat and to tell them apart from poisonous ones. Doing so is deeply reassuring and each clarification is seized upon gratefully. However, Saussure also pointed out that if we have understood that a particular food is not poisonous, we have nonetheless also come to realize that *some* food *might* be. Every signification of safety therefore creates

---

10 See F. de Saussure, 1974, *Course in General Linguistics*, London: Fontana.

alternative possibilities of danger. Establishing usage for a word is thus often accompanied by anxiety as to its correctness.

Type A language attempts to deal with this problem by creating a specific usage that rules out alternatives. To do this, it rejects various troublesome characteristics of Type B language such as emotion, bias and prejudice, humour, irony and imagery. In their place, it takes on an innocent directness, preferring the written word – which can be codified scientifically – and using it to discipline the spoken word, which is prone to vagaries of intention and desire. However, though written rules proliferate, they never succeed in taming speech, for it is in speech that language is continually reborn. In supervision, for example, we try to avoid cliché when reaching for a depth of emotional significance. The received meaning of spoken words is alive in a way that can never be entirely predictable. As Jacques Lacan has put it, 'the breadth of how I might be interpreted always exceeds the more delimited field of what I had intended to say'.[11]

By and large, the two kinds of language coexist without causing major problems because each knows its task. They also depend on one another psychologically. Off-duty doctors and policemen employ graveyard humour to compensate for the correctness of their professional language: and there comes a moment when even a committed ironist feels bound to say, 'No, but to be serious for a second ...' There are, however, occasions when one language trespasses on the territory of the other and the interesting thing to note is how immoderately angry people then become. One obvious example might be the use of improper or 'dirty' language.

An analogy may be drawn here with the anthropologist Mary Douglas's understanding of dirt as a 'taxonomic embarrassment' or 'matter out of place'.[12] In Type A language, the suspicion of impropriety occurs when the intention to sustain innocent meaning becomes compromised by emotional and ironic awareness. We can see this, for example, in the uptake and subsequent decay

---

11 J. Lacan, 2006, *Écrits*, translated by B. Fink, New York: W. W. Norton, p. 197.

12 M. Douglas, 1984, *Purity and Danger*, London: Routledge, p. 42.

of euphemistic circumlocutions such as 'challenging behaviour' (still current) or 'educationally subnormal' (discontinued).

In the case of Type B language, Douglas's taxonomical embarrassment may take the perhaps surprising form of rationality. The following incident will illustrate what I have in mind. In a recent article in *Therapy Today*, Rosemary Rizq, a chartered psychologist, described coming across a whiteboard in a consulting room on which a CBT practitioner had written of her patient's recent bereavement – 'Dysfunctional thought: my husband is dead.' Rizq considered this language to be a perversion of care, because it turned 'a blind eye to the difficulties, limitations and realities involved in working with mental distress'.[13] The regrettable way in which reason can sometimes become intrusive and actually *unreasonable* is of particular relevance to Angela's story. So with this particular instance of 'matter out of place' in mind, let us turn to it.

The situation

One day towards the end of last year, Angela came to see me for our customary monthly supervision. She works in a small team of palliative care specialists. Most of her patients have cancer. Her role has both a clinical focus in advising on medication for pain relief and a pastoral one in liaising with patients' families: many people prefer to die at home, though this is not always possible. A nurse manager is attached to the team. Jane, the current holder of this post, has an oncology background but no previous experience of palliative care.

Angela brings to supervision tensions concerning the transition from a Hippocratic culture dedicated to healing (which is ancient) and the Palliative culture (which is much more recent in our society) that recognizes and works with the doctor and the patient and *within* each of us. Determining the point at which the expectation of ongoing life gives way to the acceptance of dying

---

13 R. Rizq, 2013, 'The Language of Healthcare', *Therapy Today* 24:2, pp. 20–5, 20.

can be complex and controversial. There is often great anxiety present and many psychological defences are raised against it, as Elizabeth Kübler-Ross has shown.[14]

Presenting such transitions in supervision involves a detailed account of the progress of clinical symptoms over a period of time, something in which Angela is highly skilled. Her narratives are slow and deliberate; her recall is precise. Although I am not a medic, I find what she says accessible and often moving. Despite her extensive experience, she is not inured to the onset of dying. W. E. Henley's lines have caught the sense of incipient terror that is always to be reckoned with:

> Madame Life's a piece in bloom
>   Death goes dogging everywhere:
> She's the tenant of the room,
>   He's the ruffian on the stair.[15]

Angela's role is largely advisory. Her authority depends upon her knowledge of palliative medication, her accumulated experience of symptoms, her presence (she can spend longer than other staff with a patient or relative) and her ability to empathize. To find her voice within situations characterized by severe personal crisis, suffering and loss, she has to draw upon reserves of courage and forbearance.

We have been working together for twelve years. The supervision has an explicit pastoral understanding, supporting her both in her work and in her relations with colleagues. Some of her personal details are therefore relevant. She is forty-nine years old, the younger of two sisters, both single, who lost their father twenty-two years ago and their mother three years ago. During the previous year Angela's sister Caroline (fifty-five) had received a diagnosis of terminal cancer: her condition and her prognosis are of a kind with which Angela is familiar in her work. Caroline

---

14 See: E. Kübler-Ross, 1989, *On Death and Dying*, London: Routledge.

15 Quoted in R. Dinnage, 1992, *The Ruffian on the Stair*, London: Penguin, title page.

had been working abroad as a teacher, but returned to England at Easter; she now lives an hour's drive away.

Two years previously the management of Angela's clinic had determined that nurse specialists without a higher degree should obtain one as a condition of demonstrating their competence, upon which promotion to higher grades would depend. As a consequence, Angela began studying for an MSc. Provision of study time was initially made possible by management but was subsequently partly eroded in a round of spending cuts. Taking time to be with her sister as her health deteriorated meant that Angela fell behind in her studies over the summer. In October came a new pressure when another member of the team went on maternity leave. Reluctantly Angela decided to apply for a year's postponement of her degree. She obtained the relevant forms from her university and took them to her manager, Jane, for signature.

The event

Angela entered Jane's office wanting to obtain her support quickly and efficiently. Instead she found Jane inclined to ask questions about the MSc and answered them as patiently as she could. In talking about the next year, Jane then raised the question of Caroline's health. Somewhat taken aback, Angela told her that her sister was receiving a new drug treatment. Jane knew of this drug, and both understood that without it, Caroline would already be dead. (Angela's understanding is that Caroline's life-expectancy is nevertheless more a matter of months than years.) Based on her own understanding of the drug's effectiveness, Jane then launched into what Angela described as 'a highly inaccurate and over-optimistic prognosis' of Caroline's condition.

This made Angela extremely angry without quite knowing how or why. She responded by saying that 'one could never be certain, things could tip up quite suddenly'. Her account to me continued: 'Jane then caused my feelings to fall further into decline when she started to use the sort of terminology that we associate with a patient at high risk.' I asked her what that terminology might be.

She replied, 'Oh, how vulnerable Caroline was to septicaemia, to emboli lodging in the blood supply to one of her lungs or to her brain, or to developing painful and immobilizing fractures as a result of her bone metastases.'

Angela had listened to this without making reply. Jane then asked in conclusion, 'So her condition might undergo sudden change?' This seemingly innocuous question contained for Angela a coded meaning, established within her own practice, suggesting that her sister might now be in the very last days of her life. She was not clear whether Jane intended to imply this or not. Understandably, it caused her considerable further distress. By this point I was feeling utterly confused, yet aware that something very significant was occurring. A silence – an unusually long one – developed between us.

Our supervision meeting took place later on the day of the conversation between Angela and Jane. I sensed that something was wrong as soon as Angela entered the room. Behind her normal bustling demeanour, I saw she was more than usually hesitant and behaving with the kind of cautious introspection I associate with someone who has been deeply hurt and is trying to master her feelings.

As her story unfolded, I found myself becoming angry on her behalf – a feeling that has returned in writing this account. Jane's lack of tact and sensitivity struck me then as monstrous. I made a half-hearted and unsuccessful attempt to conceal this feeling, and Angela was, I think, momentarily grateful to see how much I cared.

However, she is a fair-minded and unflappable person and not one to over-indulge in protest, so we soon settled down to try to understand what had taken place. Given that Jane is generally known to be well-intentioned, what might explain her choice of inquiry and the abrupt way her response switched from optimism to pessimism? And what can account for the severity of the psychological wound that Angela had received?

Observations

Long before she arrived in Jane's office, Angela had clearly been faced with a gradual accumulation of threats to her comfort and safety at work. Such a stealthy piling up of challenging circumstances can easily outwit the self-protecting surveillance that an experienced carer practises out of habit: when the final straw lands, it takes them by surprise. A setback to professional identity can add to a level of anxiety that already exists about sustaining a punishing work schedule. It is therefore reasonable to suppose that present within Angela's approach to Jane was a need for support, reassurance and encouragement.

That said, Angela is not generally a needy person and she would have been satisfied with a nod, a smile and a quick signature from her manager. Why did Jane opt for a longer and more detailed conversation? As a manager, Jane is naturally concerned to follow guidelines, obey rules and establish correct procedures. However, her behaviour puzzled Angela as well as hurt her: it was out of character. Could it be that Jane sensed a quick exchange would not be sufficient?

A reason to account for a deeper level of distress in Angela, one perhaps of which she was less aware but which nevertheless made its presence felt to Jane, may be found in two instances of role confusion contained within the incident.

The first occurred when Angela was questioned about the MSc. Consideration must be given to the impact upon her of this new academic discipline, undertaken 'entirely voluntarily', as Angela put it to me, 'though under what I perceived to be a threat'. In addition to carrying out her duties, she was now expected to justify them, to a greater degree than hitherto, within the rigorous and exacting framework of evidence-based practice. This is easy enough when giving an account of clinical circumstances, but much harder when it comes to qualitative pastoral matters. Angela had to extend her nursing skills to include critical reading and writing. She had to make room within the many initiatives she already took on behalf of others for fresh and unfamiliar initiatives to satisfy the examiners. The MSc pitted her notion of herself as altruistic and possessing acquired practical wisdom against a new and unwelcome picture of herself as either ignorant or needing to summon a new kind of academic assertiveness in order to prove that she was not ignorant.

The second, far more sensitive factor was the terminal illness of her sister. The obvious aspect – that she faced the loss of the surviving member of her immediate family – may have obscured a more troubling feature. She was in role here as a responsible relative with her own considerable needs; but the circumstances will have also conjured up in her mind all the thoughts associated with nursing a patient. These would include sharing with doctors a prognosis in which careful attention to the progress of symptoms was matched by caution in drawing conclusions. In the case of a stranger, such a procedure might bring with it a certain assurance: where the patient is one's own sister, the same guessing game can become an agony – if (and it is a big if) she can allow herself to contemplate it at all.

Could it be that Jane was motivated to inquire by a subconscious sense of a lacuna, an empty space within Angela's awareness that was both inviting exploration and resisting it? Whether or not we can accept that an awkward state of loaded subliminal consciousness was shared by the two women, we do know that Jane tried to mirror Angela's feelings, but in the process over-egged her responses and found herself caught up in an oscillation that she struggled to control. 'Is it good news about your sister then?' she was saying, 'Or is it bad; *terrible* in fact?' Faced with this unstable dynamic, the solution Jane's mind hit upon was to have recourse to clinical language, the discourse of evidence-based practice and dispassionate objectivity. They discussed Angela's sister as they would a patient who was occupying a much-needed bed. How much longer would she require care? Could the release be estimated? Would this coincide with a return to study?

It was only in talking it through in supervision that it became clear to Angela that these deliberations were not what she had wanted at all. She then came to realize a source of her anger – that she had projected on to Jane some of her own guilt and dismay at betraying Caroline's intimate secrets. A meeting that simply sought a signature had become fraught when it expanded to include pastoral considerations. It was overloaded with what Angela felt to be 'matter out of place' and lacked the means to deal with it. Thoughts that needed discretion and time had been shoehorned into a single, information-sharing exchange. A decision that needed sensitivity had been handled on too rational a basis. Yet, neither woman had spoken out of malice. In attempting to avoid or minimize emotional pain, Jane had finally resorted to a language which was felt, in retrospect, to have insulted or invalidated an alternative language.

Can we mean what we say? Concluding reflections

The foregoing story raises familiar psychological questions. Can we depend upon our voice to convey with reliable accuracy the intentions of our mind: and can we say with any certainty what those intentions are? Common terms like 'hesitate' and 'blurt out' suggest we are not always in control of speech or thought. However, supervision can provide the exploratory space needed to catch up with ourselves. James Britton, whose interest is in rhetoric, has proposed that, in dramatic circumstances, meaning can be constituted at the point of utterance.[16]

Giving voice here enacts the mysterious double nature of a transitional thought – something that, in giving birth to awareness, both represents *and* enacts; both *refers to* something other and *is itself*.[17] An example might be, 'I didn't know I thought that until I heard myself saying it.' The act of speaking can sometimes release wholly new meaning in a speaker's awareness. The stimulus provided by the supervisor's sympathetic attention provides a vital ingredient of release and containment: what happens next can be a moment of pure discovery.

That said, making a statement in a tricky situation where feelings are running high is not necessarily the best or only option. The choice of silence, established by Angela and followed by me,

---

16 See: J. Britton, 1972, *Language and Learning*, Oxford: Heinemann.
17 R. M. Young, 1994, *Mental Space*, London: Process Press, p. 146.

allowed a pause for thought. It acknowledged that more was at stake than was immediately apparent. It made possible the emergence of what Owen Barfield called 'figuration' – the first inklings of an idea.[18] Silence can postpone the problematic *certainties* that a particular choice of words brings with it.

The confusion of meaning in Angela's and Jane's encounter may also be elucidated by developmental psychology. In *Women's Ways of Knowing* Mary Belenky and her colleagues described a condition of cowed voice-less-ness, to which we can all regress when dependent on the whims of a hostile external authority.[19] Here words are weapons used against us, and in using words back, we render ourselves guilty and liable to punishment. Knowledge is only of the present actuality, which is perceived to be uncompromisingly bad. Speaking about our own experience in such challenging circumstances can feel impossible, but it starts with the first frightened, tentative connection between voice, mind and self. In the next stage of Belenky's developmental scheme, Type A language becomes immensely attractive as we work hard to receive and retain what authority dictates. There is no originality to this thinking, which is intolerant of ambiguity. In time, however, we react in favour of a more subjective stance and a sense of self emerges with strong personal convictions. Type B language is now acquired and put to use. Belenky's research suggested that women at this stage distrusted logic, analysis and abstraction, seeing them as exclusively male preserves. Coming to terms with the skills of critical argument and learning how to use them belonged to the final stages of 'Procedural' and 'Constructed' knowledge, in which maturity and integration were achieved.

Belenky's account of these later developments fits well with what I know of Angela. The self-critical awareness, the subtle integration of subjective and objective viewpoints and the use of cognitive action to create emotional containment for her patients

---

18 O. Barfield, 1988, *Saving the Appearances*, Middletown, CT: Wesleyan University Press, p. 24.

19 M. Belenky, B. M. Clinchy, N. R. Goldberger, J. M. Tarule, 1997, *Women's Ways of Knowing*, New York: Basic Books.

all point to her practised handling of the two languages of denotation and suggestion, calculation and belief. But it is also possible that she and Jane regressed to earlier stages of subjectivity in their meeting, succumbing to both the prospect of grief and the desire to behave correctly. We might even describe her wounded state on entering my room as being silenced and voice-less. Belenky's research shows starkly the regression that an inhumane system of governance can induce in both women and men.

There were, finally, other psychological factors present at the meeting, not directly attributable to either Angela or Jane. Central to a *pastoral* understanding is the meaning that emerges in considering the social environment that protagonists inhabit. Readers may have noticed that, as Angela unfolded her story, I became caught up in it and allowed my feelings to show. This was not very professional of me. The useful significance of my behaviour lay, however, in the *enactment* that was present in the parallel process.

My feelings were 'matter out of place' but they were also the material with which exploration could proceed. The psychoanalyst Jacques Lacan created a model which can summarize this event by bringing together its three key elements:

- the two women
- their use of language
- the threats posed by imminent death, overwork and keeping to procedure.[20]

The model borrows a device from a celebrated Italian Renaissance family called Borromeo. It consists of three interlinked rings which hold each other together. If any one ring is broken, the whole falls apart. Each ring is taken by Lacan to represent a separate and interacting element in a conversation.

---

20 Jacques Lacan, 1975, *Le Seminaire Livre XX Encore 1972–3*, Paris: Seuil.

Figure 2: Lacan's Borromean knot

Real

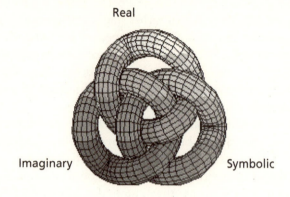

Imaginary   Symbolic

Within the *Imaginary* he included the image of a person available to the gaze, the internalized idea of a person present in phantasy, and the reflective interplay between the persons involved in mirroring and hence in projection. Here are Angela and Jane, exposed to one another by the unusual circumstance of Angela's admission of failure to cope. Here too is Angela's intimate acquaintance with her sister and Jane's suppositions about a stranger. Here are both nurses' dreams of cancerous growth. Here are the efforts Jane makes to engage with Angela that then go so badly astray.

Second, Lacan introduced the *Symbolic*, an equally large term by which he understood the sources of meaningful communication in signifiers, codes, language and law. Here is the role that each woman occupied with all that it denoted. Here is the code of professional conduct that governed their behaviour towards one another. Here are the two languages, each with its proper sphere of usage. Here is the unspoken law that forbids intrusive enquiry about a person's private life.

Third, beyond the reach of all appearances and communication, Lacan placed what he called the *Real*. This is *so real* (and hence potentially threatening) that Lacan suggested it can only exist as a gap in a representation, a repressed truth, and a moment when the shortcomings of apparent certainty become evident.

Taken as a whole, the model enables us to examine the nature of the enactment. It was a crisis in which various factors in Angela's life that had long been building, all came together. If the ring of the *Imaginary* had been broken, it would have meant the two women had fallen out. Their working relationship would have also suffered (the *Symbolic*) and they would have denied themselves insight into how it had happened (the *Real*). It was, however, the ring of the *Symbolic* that did get ruptured, at least with regard to the inopportune use of language: it was a partial breakage because Angela and Jane succeeded in remaining within the required codes of the clinic's etiquette. The scandal of the mis-used language left a lasting impression on Angela, however, and it was actually in the supervision with me – my inability to control my reaction – that a breaking open of the *Real* occurred.

Conclusion

Like so many other attempts to alert us to potential threat, the term 'verbal abuse' has become sadly worn and tired of late. I hope I have nonetheless managed to convey the quite extraordinary violence that was done to Angela, albeit by a well-meaning colleague. The rough and ready characterization of two kinds of language that I have attempted may, I hope, help to clarify how such grievous misunderstandings can arise. Angela, meanwhile, is coming for supervision again later today. Her sister continues to enjoy life and Angela's work as a nurse still provides her with rich satisfaction. It now lies within the practical wisdom she has acquired from experience to restore what has been damaged within her.

PART TWO

Reflections on Practice

5

Supervision as Courageous Conversation: A Supervisor's Reflections

TONY NOLAN

Power and vulnerability, courage and risk are shared realities for both supervisor and supervisee. In this chapter, a pastoral supervisor explores how acknowledging and embracing those realities has the potential to change supervision from a box-ticking requirement of professional practice into an opportunity for transformational learning and renewal.

What is behind the notion that supervision requires courage? And what is it about this process that invites us into the realm of risk? As supervisees, supervision requires taking a chance that a supervisor will accept us, support us and challenge us – and invite us to be the best we can be, no matter what the work or ministry. Paradoxically, the same invitation – to risk, to take a chance, to be the best we can be – is offered to the supervisor. The dimensions of the invitation to both supervisee and supervisor become evident in the supervisory relationship. They both learn, grow, change and are stretched in conversation with each other. The key to this being possible lies in the working alliance.

This chapter is a reflection on my experience as a supervisor who is also a supervisee. I have received supervision for more than fifteen years, and that experience has coloured and flavoured my practice as a supervisor. As a supervisee I know how it is to be challenged, cared for, supported and 'rebalanced' in my relationship with my ministry. As a supervisor my desire is to offer similar opportunities to those with whom I come in contact.

Supervision, at its heart, is a courageous conversation, and courage by definition involves the heart; to give heart to another is to *encourage*. It takes courage to seek out a supervisor and to be willing to open your world and practice to the objective gaze of another. It also takes courage to enter into an alliance in which exploration, challenge and some elements of evaluation are implicit. For supervisors, too, it takes courage to remain true to their highest aspirations in terms of practice, to acknowledge their biases, and to enter an alliance that places them at the service of their supervisees. And it also takes courage for supervisors to invite feedback: to engage with supervisees in a way that invites evaluation of the supervisor's practice. Supervision that is courageous is ready to take such feedback on board and willing to act on it.

So, if supervision is a 'conversation of the heart' that attends to the work practice as well as the emotional impact of that work on the supervisee, how can I as a supervisor best serve the supervisee and the process? How can I remain flexible, responsive and imaginative in a relationship that seeks to support ethical and creative practice in both supervisee and supervisor? These questions draw me towards three aspects of supervision that reflect its courageous quality:

- The courage to see with new eyes. How do I enter a relationship with my supervisees that offers them a liberating view of their pastoral work and pastoral relationships?
- The courage to name the unnoticed. How do I support supervisees to become aware of and attend to, the 'less than obvious' – the peripheral, barely noticed elements of work?
- The courage to ask for what you want. How do I facilitate the development of a supervisory relationship that is open and clear and offers a well-negotiated working alliance?

The courage to see with new eyes

In supervision generally, a more experienced practitioner is available to a less experienced practitioner to discuss the latter's work and its impact on them, and to support them in the planning and doing of this work. The experience of being supervised is often positive and enriching, providing a balance of support and challenge that encourages reflection and prompts the supervisee towards excellence in practice. In some quarters, however, supervision is met with distrust and anxiety: it has come to mean micro-management, judgement, shame and failure. There is some debate about the value of renaming the practice we now call supervision in an effort to make it more palatable. The difficulty, however, lies not in the word but in the assumptions, interpretations and poor practices that have sometimes grown up around it. It is therefore important to reclaim the true meaning of supervision.

In attempting to see with new eyes, the supervisor attends to the professional needs of the supervisee as well as to the work and the manner in which it is undertaken. Crucially, this endeavour to see also applies to the supervisee's inner processes, including their experience of themselves in the work as well as their shifting perceptions of these events and encounters.

Michael Carroll describes supervision as a way of seeing things differently, literally applying a 'super-vision' that brings new eyes, new perceptions and new vision to the work: a super way of visioning.[1] This is what Bolton imaginatively describes as the 'hawk in the mind' and Scaife 'thinking with a birds-eye view' about an event or aspect of practice.[2] This 'super' way of seeing prompts new meanings and wider understandings of experience. Hawkins' and Shohet's 'seven-eyed' model of supervision also

---

1 M. Carroll, 2010, 'Supervision: a Journey of Lifelong Learning', in R. Shohet (ed.), *Supervision as Transformation: A Passion for Learning*, London: Jessica Kingsley, pp. 14–28.

2 For both these ideas see: J. Scaife, 2010, *Supervising the Reflective Practitioner: An Essential Guide to Theory and Practice*, Abingdon: Routledge, p. 3.

evokes this dimension of the process, encouraging a view of the work that holds many perspectives or windows.[3]

This super-vision involves being prepared to take on new ways of seeing. In pastoral contexts particularly, supervision is often perceived as a space in which work or ministry is discussed, and logical thinking and planning are applied to particular difficulties or dilemmas. While this is, in fact, often the practice of supervision and can work very well, we also need to broaden the potential of supervision to include a variety of learning styles, engaging creatively and imaginatively with the process. Sometimes words are not enough – as Mooli Lahad reminds us:

> The use of metaphors, stories, images and similar expressive media, whether in the therapeutic or in the supervision process, is based on the assumption that a story or image can represent the objective or subjective perception of internal or external reality.[4]

One creative approach is through stories, which can illustrate a feature of practice in a way that is accessible (and sometimes humorous) for supervisees. They appeal to the imagination and supervisees often come to see story, parable or metaphor as a resource in their own work. One of Grimms' fairy tales, 'The Twelve Windows', captures for me the essence of supervision and demonstrates a new way of seeing. Like every good story it begins by focusing on time, space and context:

> Once upon a time there lived a princess who had a marvellous talent. She had such keen eyesight that nothing, no matter how small, could go undetected by her gaze. To practise this remarkable gift, the princess had a special room constructed in the tallest tower of the castle. The room had twelve windows, from which the princess could see the whole kingdom. Many young men came to seek her hand in marriage. To each she set

---

3 See P. Hawkins and R. Shohet, 2012, *Supervision in the Helping Professions*, 4th edn, Maidenhead: Open University Press.

4 M. Lahad, 2000, *Creative Supervision*, London: Jessica Kingsley, p. 15.

the same challenge, to hide in a place where she could not see them. Each suitor was given three chances. Though many tried none succeeded in hiding from her magical gaze.

One day a young shepherd came to the castle determined to win the princess's hand in marriage. She gave him the same three chances to hide. The first and the second time the princess discovered him easily. For the third and final time, she climbed the tower to the room with the twelve windows. As she climbed the steps she spotted a beautiful white cat sitting outside the room. She picked the cat up and placed it on her shoulder, little realising it was the young man in disguise. The cat curled around her neck as the princess looked through each window in turn. She was thrilled when having gazed through each window the young man could not be found anywhere in the kingdom. At that moment the cat jumped down from her shoulder and with a flash of golden light turned back into the young shepherd.[5]

This story goes to the heart of the supervisory process: the wider gaze and broader view of the world which come from the supervisor's invitation: 'Show me your world – help me see what it is like to be you in this work.' A core element of supervision is the capacity to see the world through the eyes of the supervisee and to see it bigger, more broadly. The story reminds me that by entering the world of supervisees, I am also entering the world beyond them: the world of the community they serve.

The other crucial element in the story is that for the princess, although each window provides a particular view of her world, something is missing: something remains unseen. This is the cat perched upon her shoulder (in fact the man she seeks, in disguise). The very thing she is searching for eludes her gaze: it is so close to her that she misses it. Likewise, an important aspect of supervision is paying attention to blind-spots, the unnoticed elements in us and in the work that impact on the way we engage in ministry.

---

5 This is the story as told by Walter de la Mare, 1968, *Tales Told Again*, London: Faber & Faber, with some small changes made by the author of this chapter.

This also offers the opportunity to widen our vision to greater and more imaginative possibilities in the way we work.

The courage to name the unnoticed

Several writers on supervision have explored the skill of encouraging and helping the supervisee to 'bring the work into the room'.[6] This is essential, but it may be impeded by conscious and unconscious features of both supervisor and supervisee. Like the cat perched on the princess's shoulder, the work may already be in the room, resting unnoticed on the periphery of the supervisee's awareness. A supervisee may need help to name and attend to these realities. It is attending to such phenomena that makes the learning in supervision truly transformative.

In order for this to happen it is important for the supervisor to invite the supervisee into a space that is encouraging and makes room for risk. This is partly achieved by what Davys and Beddoe describe as a 'supervision ritual' – activities and gestures by which we mark the opening and closing of the supervisory encounter.[7] For example, in my own practice, I offer my supervisees a cup of tea or coffee before each session, and this is influenced by my family and cultural identity, which place value on hospitality. Supervisees appreciate the gesture. There is something both relaxing and reassuring about holding a mug of tea, especially when you are new and unsure how to proceed.

It also gives the supervisee an opportunity to 'land', to settle and gather their thoughts. We all enter the supervisory space in different ways. Some people arrive and immediately present their work, appearing to know what they want and how to articulate it. Others need a few minutes to 'warm up', as one supervisee called it. As I write this, I am sure some readers are thinking

---

6 See, for example, Jane Leach and Michael Paterson, 2010, *Pastoral Supervision: A Handbook*, London: SCM Press; Van Ooijen, 2003, *Clinical Supervision Made Easy*, London: Churchill Livingstone; A. Davys and L. Beddoe, 2010, *Best Practice in Professional Supervision: A Guide for the Helping Professions*, London: Jessica Kingsley.

7 Davys and Beddoe, *Best Practice*, p. 93.

'What a waste of time' or even that I am colluding with reluctant supervisees. Perhaps. For me, however, these five or so minutes of a ninety-minute session offer an opportunity to attend to supervisees who value a warming-up period. There is a chance for them to catch their breath, focus on the task ahead and adopt a reflective posture. This is important, since it communicates that I am willing to be flexible, that I am focused on their needs and that I am interested in them as a person as well as a practitioner. It helps build a sense of trust, safety and being valued.

A second important help to naming the unnoticed is a contemplative attitude to supervision. According to Maureen Conroy, supervision needs to be 'primarily contemplative and evocative if the supervisee is to develop a discerning heart'.[8] The supervisor's task is to create a space that will allow a supervisee's inner and professional life to unfold in its own way.

Similarly, Sheila Ryan argues that supervision needs to be built on a posture of 'mindfulness which encourages us to base our actions upon our real embodied experiences'. For Ryan, this mindful approach, which pays close attention to what we ourselves are experiencing, is key to getting below the surface. She goes on to suggest that by adopting a contemplative stance in supervision we are not simply taking what is presented on face value but are looking with interest and curiosity into all that is, including what we have edited out of our stories; that is, the aspects of the work deemed too embarrassing, trivial, useless or frightening.[9] This kind of respectful curiosity is the hallmark of the good supervisor.

Indeed, it is mindful attention that encourages me to gaze with equal curiosity on the supervisee's named issue for the session and their throwaway comments, especially at the beginning of the session. The latter brings us back to the princess with the cat on her shoulder. For example, I notice remarks made by the supervisee before or as we settle into the space and wonder if these will play out in the session. Sometimes comments and images appear

---

8 M. Conroy, 1995, *Looking into the Well: Supervision of Spiritual Directors*, Chicago: Loyola Press, p. 40.

9 S. Ryan, 2008, 'Mindful Supervision', in R. Shohet (ed.), 2008, *Passionate Supervision*, London: Jessica Kingsley, pp. 80–110.

to have been 'parked', waiting like a well-worn suitcase to be collected as they leave.

Some clergy, in particular, find it difficult to name those issues in ministry with which they struggle. More often than not, however, these make themselves known through small hints that get dropped into the conversation as they arrive, almost as though the supervisee is saying indirectly, 'I want to talk about this issue but I don't know how to bring it into supervision, so I drop hints, hoping the supervisor will hear and respond.' As a supervisor, if I am looking with interest to all that transpires within the supervisory process, that looking – that 'hawk in the mind' – must include a willingness to notice and name what lies on the edge of our vision, on the periphery. To return to our story, the cat is that something curled around the supervisee's shoulder, sufficiently out of their sight to be easily missed. Looking at this with curiosity, inviting it into the supervisee's awareness, can bring new insight.

If we do not attend to what unconsciously enters the supervision space as well as what the supervisee consciously brings, we may find that what the supervisee really wants to explore remains unseen and an important learning opportunity can be lost. In other words, the supervisor needs to listen carefully for what Hawkins and Shohet call the hidden 'connecting patterns'.[10]

There is a further aspect to mindful supervision: that supervisors listen to supervisees and at the same time attend to the impact of the listening on themselves. Supervisors need to distinguish between their own internal process and that of the supervisee.

For the supervisor, naming the unnoticed is risky and requires courage. They may be wondering, 'What if I am wrong?' 'What will the supervisee think of me?' 'Will they engage with this insight?' 'Will they feel unheard or that my "wisdom" is being forced on them?' Equally, the supervisee requires courage to engage in this shift in the process. For both of them to risk the emergent in the session, to risk attending to the here and now, indicates something of the level of trust and safety that exists in the supervisory

---

10 Hawkins and Shohet, *Supervision in the Helping Professions*, p. 91.

relationship, and whether the relationship is experienced as safe enough for the supervisee to engage with what has been pushed to the edge of sight. *Can* the cat on the shoulder that remains just beyond our peripheral vision be seen and named for what it is?

This was certainly my experience when working with Roger, a curate in the Church of England, who had been coming to see me for several years. On this particular occasion, as he entered the room he mentioned a scene from a movie he had watched the previous evening and then quickly moved on to the issue he wished to bring to supervision. However, as we explored the supervisory issue, I became increasingly aware that the movie scene kept finding its way back into my thoughts. It seemed to me that it hovered on the edge of our conversation, waiting to be seen, invited in and given a voice. I decided to share with Roger what I was experiencing:

> You know, Roger, I find the image you shared at the beginning of our time together keeps coming back into my mind. I'm wondering if we were to invite it back into the conversation what insight it might shed on what we are presently reflecting on. How would that be for you?

Roger was willing. By inviting the image back into the conversation some powerful insights emerged for him, including an awareness that the forceful style of his training incumbent was undermining his self-confidence, leaving him feeling de-skilled and voiceless.

Supervision, then, is most effective when the supervisee feels that the supervisor can be trusted not to shame or judge them. The supervisor's role is to provide a sheltering sky under which the supervisee can safely explore their work, unburden themself and attend to the more difficult and stretching aspects of practice.

The courage to ask for what you want

Building the working alliance encourages openness and trust, and supports a clear boundary in the work. For some, asking for what they want is not easy: it demands openness, honesty and willingness to name what each needs and expects from the other. This can be a challenge and is in itself an act of courage.

The courage to ask for what you want is also something that the supervisor's approach can help to make possible. It is important throughout the supervisory relationship, but perhaps nowhere more so than:

- in setting up the contract or working alliance
- if disagreements occur
- as the relationship comes to an end.

Setting up the working alliance

It is my practice to provide new supervisees with a written copy of the working alliance before our first session, so that they can jot down any thoughts they have about it before we meet. The key issues that need exploring at this stage are discussed in some detail in Leach's and Paterson's *Pastoral Supervision: A Handbook*, so I will only add a few comments here.[11]

A key issue in setting up the contract is how we understand confidentiality. As someone who also provides spiritual direction, I have on many occasions heard other directors say that they do not negotiate confidentiality with their directees, opting instead for a general statement that whatever is shared is considered confidential. This raises important questions, such as: what happens if someone shares information that cannot legally be held confidentially? Tschudin suggests that at the outset supervision must attend to the 'ethics of confidentiality'.[12] With this in mind, I ask

---

11 Leach and Paterson, *Pastoral Supervision*, pp. 21–8.

12 Cited in A. Epling and P. Cassedy, 2001, 'Clinical Supervision: Visions from the Classroom', in J. R. Cutcliffe, T. Butterworth and B. Proctor (eds), *Fundamental Themes in Clinical Supervision*, London: Routledge, p. 76.

questions such as 'What does confidentiality mean to you?' and 'What is confidential material?' This helps us both flesh out our understanding through concrete examples. We then compose a shared definition, one that acknowledges both personal and legal responsibility.

A consideration of confidentiality sows the seeds for defining boundaries, building trust and the appropriate use of power. For example, one supervisee responded to the question, 'What will make this space safe?' by saying, 'We meet in a friendly atmosphere but not as friends, and only in the context of the work.' This made it clear for both of us that this was to be a purposeful, focused and limited connection.

Having defined our common understanding of confidentiality and articulated our needs in terms of safety and trust-building, we can move on to discuss the goals, tasks and parameters of the supervisory relationship. This clarifies the content and our mutually understood expectations of supervision as well as identifying assumptions regarding the roles of supervisor and supervisee.

It also enables me to challenge any aspects of their expectations that do not accord with my own. For example, Malcolm was a priest in a busy city parish. Having completed a training course in spiritual direction, he found that he was being asked more and more for spiritual direction and approached me for supervision. Our initial exploratory conversation went well, and Malcolm expressed willingness to work together, so we set a date to discuss our working alliance. As we began to negotiate, it became clear that Malcolm's previous experience of supervision (within the training course) had not been a happy one.

As we reflected on the purpose of supervision and Malcolm's goals, it became obvious that his negative experience of supervision had coloured his understanding of the process, leaving him anxious and lacking in confidence. It had instilled in him a perception of the supervisor as the wise expert whose role was to critique his practice and correct perceived mistakes. Through our discussion, some of his anxieties were alleviated.

Disagreements and disputes

The trust that is built up in the relationship is needed in particular when 'mistakes' require to be acknowledged by either side, or there are disagreements or disputes between supervisor and supervisee. Disputes may occur when the supervisor misunderstands the supervisee or intervenes in a way that is experienced as insensitive or prying. If this is not addressed, it may cause an abrupt and unresolved ending. It is important that both parties acknowledge when the contract is not working well.

In my experience it is easier to manage disagreement if the supervisee and I have discussed such a possibility at the beginning of our work together. It can be helpful to agree to disclose and discuss any sense of dissonance as soon as there is an awareness of some disagreement, and I sometimes ask supervisees how I will know if they are angry, unhappy, disheartened with our contact. By bringing this into the open, we acknowledge that it may happen and allow for it to be part of the work of supervision. This conversation also provides an opportunity to introduce the concept of mutual feedback. It is usual for the supervisee to expect feedback as part of the work together, but it is equally important for the supervisee to be willing to give feedback to the supervisor.

Ending

Ending a supervisory relationship is as delicate a process as its beginning and, again, this has been discussed in some detail in Leach and Paterson.[13] Wherever possible, a planned ending is preferable, one that includes the personal rituals we associate with ending. It is a good opportunity to reflect on the work done and the critical learning for both supervisor and supervisee.

---

13 Leach and Paterson, *Pastoral Supervision*, ch. 8.

Conclusions

What then of my experience as a supervisor? We each experience the world in a particular and unique way. Supervision challenges me to listen, to imagine, and attend to the particular and unique world of the supervisee. It demands that I suspend some of my familiar and comfortable assumptions and offers a particular way of learning from the inside out. I find myself stretched as I confront the part of myself that resists change, the part that is attached to certain beliefs and assumptions. Supervision exposes me to a world that is rich in resources and creativity and to people who model a way of work and ministry that inspires me. When they demonstrate the courage to see with new eyes, the courage to name the unnoticed and the courage to ask for what they want, I myself am encouraged.

6

A Blessing for All Those Whom, in God's Name, You Should Love: A Supervisee's Journey

LINDA J. DUNBAR

In this chapter, Linda Dunbar, a minister of the Church of Scotland (the 'Kirk'), combines the metaphor of communion with the narrative methodology of autoethnography to reflect upon her experience of supervision. Autoethnography has been described as 'an approach to research and writing that seeks to describe and systematically analyse (graphy) personal experience (auto) in order to understand cultural experience (ethno)'.[1] This essay, then, is both a product for the reader, and a process for the writer.

Be gentle when you touch bread
Let it not lie uncared for, unwanted
So often bread is taken for granted
There is so much beauty in bread
Beauty of sun and soil
Beauty of patient toil
Winds and rain have caressed it
Christ so often blessed it
Be gentle when you touch bread
Celtic Verse – anonymous

---

1 C. Ellis, T. E. Adams and A. P. Bochner, 2011, 'Autoethnography: An Overview', *Forum for Qualitative Research* 12:1, www.qualitativeresearch.net/index.php/fqs/article/view/1589/3095#

Counselling as precursor to supervision

My experience of counselling began after struggling for over a year with a growing realization that my understanding of parish ministry was irreconcilable with the church I served. Frustration, despair and mounting confusion of where God was and what was my true call within the church had seen me meet with the Kirk's Pastoral Adviser, their pastor to the pastors. It was he who suggested I should seek help, and he gave me the contact details of one of the Kirk's Ministries Counselling Schemes, a small group of professional, independent counsellors. In the event, my counselling experience lasted just over a year, extended by six or so months after my world was further disrupted by my dad's diagnosis with terminal lung cancer with a three-month prognosis. In the event, my dad lived for a further three years. Three months after his diagnosis I moved to serve a new community, and at the time of writing I happily continue in the same charge.

When my counselling ended, I made a smooth transition to monthly supervision sessions with the same person, which continues to this day. While such a switch in relationship from counsellor to supervisor in not typical, neither is it unique. In this instance, the possibility of changing from counselling to supervision was discussed for some time, and there was a negotiation of new roles and boundaries over three or four months. The switch, when it came, was straddled with a time gap and saw the major focus of the sessions change from family to work – but a thread of call and relationship remained constant. From my perspective, the process remained unchanged – perhaps because the process recognized my personality and idiosyncrasies.

The counselling journey

On the night he was betrayed

How many times have I repeated the words, 'On the night he was betrayed', within communion services? It is a piece of code for the 'in-crowd'. No mention of Judas, of gardens, shouts in the dark, soldiers, drawn swords, silver, kisses, arrest. Just six, bland words. The Words of Institution assume the hearers know the back story. I have never consciously 'explained' the back story during a communion service. I too assume prior knowledge.

On making the first of my hour-long journeys to meet my counsellor I don't know what to expect. Part of me feels a failure at not being able to cope. Part of me feels I was 'betrayed' on the night I was interviewed for the parish: I wrongly believed common dreams and visions had been shared. Part of me feels protective of my back story.

Can you drink the cup I drink? (Mark 10.38)

I arrive early enough to find the address – up a side lane with a bright red gate – and I walk right past, never pausing, never looking to the side, but continue up the narrow lane. I am scouting the lie of the land. I am nervous and fearful of what lies beyond this gate. As the appointed hour arrives, having circled the quiet streets, I come back down the lane, open the red gate and ring the bell. My body has arrived – but I'm not sure about my heart and soul.

Your book-lined room brings a degree of ease – a sign, to me, of professionalism: this is the workplace of a seeker of knowledge and understanding. Will you hold the key to my understanding of myself?

After the exchange of pleasantries, I begin the paradoxical art of dancing at a distance – being open and honest enough that there is some depth to the exchanges, but being closed enough that I feel safe from my fear of the interpretation and judgement of another. You are a stranger to me and this distance helps me feel safe. 'Can you drink the cup I drink?' Or will you gag and spit it out?

I remember a communion service in a tiny island church that had not had a minister for two years. As the half dozen communicants passed the common cup around, I drank last. My immediate desire was to spit the foul liquid from my mouth. I resisted that, but have no doubt that as I struggled to swallow, my contorted features were clear to see. At the end of the service, the dregs of the common cup were frugally poured back into the old wine bottle, the cork put on top, and the bottle returned to the cupboard, perhaps for another two years.

My efforts at that communion to continue as if nothing had happened were pitiful. Who was I kidding? I felt poisoned from such an unexpected source.

If your features contort as I share my life story, my life blood, what will I do? They say you can build up a tolerance to poisons if you imbibe them in small quantities, so I will give you small sips – and I will carefully study your response.

The Lord Jesus ... took bread, and when he had given thanks, he broke it

I recount scenes from my life story – no gagging. I try to explain my understanding of ministry – no grimacing. I garble out my hurts – no shock. Little by little over the months I hand you parts of my story. There is no particular order or logic, just whatever my flitting mind alights upon. As you sit relaxed and open in your wicker chair, you take each of my offerings in turn. You give thanks. You hold them in chaliced hands, not snatching or holding tight – for that would bruise and leave a mark. My offerings lie always open to view and available for me to take back any time I wish.

From your perspective, you can see what I can't. You can see that I have melded unrelated memories, thoughts and feelings – and then puzzled as to why they made no sense, or had jagged edges that stick out and hurt. But far from chastising me over my ill-knitted seams, you elevate my random offerings to the light shining through the window at my back. Lifting them above the shadow I cast before myself, you turn them slowly in the sunlight to enable me to see other sides, other facets I have never noticed. You ask what I see and point out where the unnatural fusions are. You ask questions. 'What does young Linda think?'

'What did young Linda feel then?' 'What would old Linda say to young Linda?' You invite me to question the aptness of some of the bonds I made years ago. And simply by your questioning, some bonds break.

This is my body …

I am very conscious that every time I enter this sanctuary I enter a thin place. As time goes on, and my trust in you (and in me?) builds, the paradoxical dancing lessens. Rather than a dinner dance, it becomes just a dinner, a simple meal of bread and wine, pain and suffering and death … And yet, this room is also a place of resurrection. This is my body, my mind, my thoughts, my feelings, my hurts and they *are* an acceptable offering to God. He does not require of me the burnt offering of my life. Rather he wants what is good for me: to act justly, to love mercy towards myself as much as others, and to walk humbly with him. He wants me to journey.

… which is broken for you

As I journey, you accept and honour my brokenness. You don't try to mend me even when, like Zuzu with her fallen petals, I long for you to 'fix' me.[2] How many times have you asked me 'What are you thinking?', and I respond that 'I want you to tell me what to do … but I know you're not going to do that', and we laugh. I steel myself to continue the task of choosing my own way.

Like the sharing of bread at communion this is a two-way exchange. You do not assume a priestly role or force me into passive receptivity. We both give and receive. You accept and honour my brokenness each time I offer it. You give me space to comprehend. There is never a rush to drown out the stillness of the ticking wall-clock. When the quietness is eventually broken you invite me to receive, in a new light, my broken pieces from your

---

2 In the film, *It's a Wonderful Life*, young Zuzu's rose has lost some of its petals, and she hands them over to her dad, pleading for him to 'fix it, Daddy'.

chaliced hands, and hold them in my own, enabling me to own them without fear or favour.

Do this in remembrance

You ask questions of my memory. 'Where have you gone?' you ask, gently drawing me back to the present when my mind has left your room and journeyed to a far-off, forgotten place. One question prompts a raft of insights, as I make links between events and thoughts separated by decades. I am not 'fixed', but I am re-membered. My disjointed memories and emotions are returned to their rightful context, viewed from a new perspective and re-ordered. You teach me the importance of memory – not by rigid rote learning, but by a process of osmosis. You teach me the importance of noticing. 'Just notice', you say. That has become a powerful mantra for my sanity. The simple act of consciously registering a memory or a feeling has provided keys to upper rooms that have long forgotten how to provide hospitality. I began this journey assuming (hoping?) I would end it with a biography, beautifully penned and proof read by another who would delete all my errors. But you are not a biographer. Instead I have an ongoing autobiography, handwritten on myriad media where each blot and stain holds memory and tells part of my story.

A new covenant: from counselling to supervision

In the same way ... he took the cup, saying, 'This cup is the new covenant'

After almost a year, I feel re-membered, but I am still on a journey. The experience of counselling surprised me in the ways it equipped me for my journey. I am a changed person, but in an 'after the fact' rather than a conscious way. My journey at home and at work still passes through night-time gardens, companions still sleep when I ask them to keep wake with me. In many ways my circumstances have not changed – but I have changed. I find myself looking back on situations almost not recognizing the 'me' who dealt with them, the things I have done and said and coped with which, just a year previously, would have rocked me to the core. Now there is a hidden assurance at my core, not of my making and not even at my command – just there, visible only in hindsight. It is time for a new covenant. It is time for a switch from counselling to supervision.

From where I stand, the mechanics of this new supervision covenant seem little different from the mechanics of counselling. The focus has changed but the tools and techniques feel very similar – the new perspectives, the giving and receiving, the journeying. It still feels like a dinner – but now I bring wine and bread of my choosing. Sometimes I bring a substantial rye bread, sometimes a light loaf. Sometimes I bring a sparkling rosé, sometimes a heady dessert wine.

Whenever you drink this, do it in remembrance

My theological tradition has no practice of reserving the sacrament. The bread and wine of each supervision session are not locked safely away in some elaborate box for use in the month ahead. What I have learned in supervision is how to consecrate the meal anew each time life or pastoral work requires it.

After nearly two years of regular supervision I have negotiated many times of crisis in work and at home. I have learned the value of exercising memory and I have learned how to cup my own hands, elevating what comes to gain a new perspective. I have learned to be gentle with myself and to know what causes me to bruise. More and more I navigate situations myself, by memory of skills and mantras and past validations. I 'notice' a lot about myself and my reactions, and that gives me control and choice about whether to continue with them or to depart from them. I never thought that two words, 'just notice', could be so powerful.

Once I was a co-celebrant at a Taizé service in an Episcopalian church. Too much port wine had been consecrated, leaving my colleague and me to consume it on empty stomachs. The joy of the communion was lost in the growing queasiness as each succeeding draft of wine was imbibed. In my supervision sessions I do not have to consume every last drop – although I am encouraged to consume more than the merest sip of wine which the tradition of individual cups has fostered.

In a recent supervision session, I wanted to serve a heady dessert wine, laid down during my dad's death, for discussion. At the last moment I became fearful that I did not have the stomach for it and opted for a sparkling rosé instead.

But you have good eyesight, and you spot the other bottle. For the next dinner, I am to email the wine list in advance, detailing what I want to discuss, and you will help me to stick to it. Come the day, I still carry two bottles, and present the rosé first. But like a good wine waiter you ask, 'What about your dad?' That particular wine, diluted with tears, took more than one session to consume.

The Blessing

I am a convert to supervision.

Supervision is a blessing to me in terms of my health. I am stronger in mind, body and spirit because of it. I am better skilled at negotiating challenges, often over-estimating the negative impact they will have on me. Without supervision I suspect I would have left ministry.

Supervision is a blessing to me in terms of the permission it gives me to take time for myself. Because of distances travelled, supervision takes a full half day out of my working month. A dawn drive through open countryside and low settled mist on the hills refreshes this city dweller no end. It is always a half day well spent. The spin-offs in terms of focus and direction for subsequent work are clear.

Supervision is a blessing to me as a thin place, a place of encounter with God and with myself. I always end a Sunday service with the words:

The blessing of almighty God, whom we call Father, Son and Holy Spirit be with you and with all those whom you love, and all those whom, in God's name, you should love.

I first heard this blessing from a neighbouring minister in Fife. It was as though a sword had pierced my heart: 'the blessing of almighty God be with all those whom in God's name I should love'. In my experience clerics do not often feel that way: we don't love ourselves. I am better at that now – sometimes.

Postscript

When she read this my supervisor commented:

For ministers, and I would suggest for many others in the caring professions, often the only tool of the trade is ourselves and our compassion. We need to care for our tools if we wish to continue to use them well in our work.

Supervision is a blessing for me, but it is also a blessing for the people among whom I work – for all those whom in God's name I should love. Because of it, because I am cared for, I am able to enter more deeply into communion with them. As I am held in my calling, I am able to receive from them, and they from me.

7

Encountering Freedom through Supervision

DAVID CARROLL

This chapter is a lightly edited version of an article, 'The Ministry of Supervision', which first appeared in 2010 in The Furrow: A Journal for the Contemporary Church *61:3, p. 152. It is printed here with the permission of the Editor of* The Furrow.

Richard Gula begins his book *Ethics in Pastoral Ministry* with an account of a man who, after pursuing a successful professional career, studied for priesthood and was ordained. A year later he met Gula and spoke of the unprofessional character of priesthood: 'There's no accountability out there!'

An immediate response from priests or religious might be the temptation to point out the differences between the vocational life and professional career. Nevertheless, as Gula rightly points out, this newly ordained priest raised a question that demands an answer:

> The attitude seems to be that having a 'religious' vocation exempts us from being held accountable to professional standards. How long will this attitude and practice go unchallenged?[1]

From my own life and experience of priesthood I know that this belief – and practice – is very real. The notion of accountability and reviewing the practice of ministry meets with resistance among many who are engaged in ministry. The recent Ryan and

---

1 R. Gula, 1996, *Ethics in Pastoral Ministry*, New York: Paulist Press, p. 1.

Murphy reports on abuse carried out by Roman Catholic priests in Dublin present a very clear picture of the consequences of the lack of accountability in ministry: it can result in harm being done to the people whom we, as ministers, are called to serve. I often hear people involved in ministry, lay and ordained, saying that they bring it to the Lord in prayer, and that is enough. When I talk of my work as a supervisor, reactions are not always positive, and as with many things of which we are unsure, the biggest reaction is that of fear.

I honestly believe that supervision is part of the response to the question raised by the priest in his conversation with Gula and that we who are engaged in pastoral ministry ought to come to see supervision itself as a ministry and one that is a necessity rather than a luxury. Jesus himself offered what could be called a model of supervision to the disciples, and we will return to this. At the same time, I understand completely the fear and nervousness of those who have not experienced the ministry and practice of supervision.

Supervision – the very word itself conjures an image of Big Brother watching over us as we go about our work. It is important to engage in defining supervision of ministry so that we will overcome the negative images. Some call it pastoral supervision, some theological reflection, and there is much literature that offers definitions of supervision. One that I particularly like is that offered by Kenneth Pohly:

> Pastoral Supervision is a method of doing and reflecting on ministry in which a supervisor (teacher) and one or more supervisees (learners) covenant together to reflect critically on their ministry as a way of growing in self-awareness, ministering competence, theological understanding, and Christian commitment.[2]

This is a layered and spiritual understanding of supervision and one that greatly informs my own ministry as a supervisor. To

---

2 K. Pohly, 2001, *Transforming the Rough Places: The Ministry of Supervision*, 2nd edn, Franklin: Providence House Publishers, pp. 107–8.

explain this, I will give a potted biography of my own ministry and experiences of supervision.

My own journey in ministry and supervision

When I was ordained in 1992, I believed that I was completely formed and ready to change the world. After a few months in my first parish, that notion of completeness was already being unpicked, and a certain amount of drifting was taking place. My experience as a newly ordained priest went un-examined and un-reflected. I do not blame anyone in particular for that; the onus was on myself to be responsible, and that was the way it had been, the way it was – and why not the way it should be ever more?

Our diocese did provide a residential course each year for those who had been ordained for ten years or less: this was part of our ongoing formation. There was a strong resistance among the group to having to attend or seeing the benefits of attending. By this time the seeds of lack of accountability were sown, and I reaped the harvest as the years went by. Like many other priests and religious, I kept saying 'Yes' to all the requests to join whatever committee or project or whatever was going on; at one stage I was one of the diocesan catechetical advisers, presenting marriage preparation courses and on the ACCORD national executive council as well as being a part-time chaplain in the local secondary school and working full-time in a parish.

This inability to say 'No' took a toll on energy, on health and on ministry: in 2004 I informed my bishop that I was leaving. I received great support from him, from family, friends and a number of close colleagues. The sense of relief was huge, and I was certain that I was doing the right thing, even though this decision was one that I took alone.

Over the course of the next twelve months I took a holiday and then began working in London in a 'real' job. I had also promised myself that I would talk with someone to reflect on my life, ministry and decisions that had brought me to this point, and a friend suggested that I attend supervision. I had encountered supervision twice before: during a Clinical Pastoral Education (CPE) course in Cork just before ordination and during a year of study in All Hallows College in Dublin. They were two very different experiences but both awakened an interest in the work of supervision, and I was open to the benefits of the process. I attended three sessions, and this reflection during my break from ministry had an enormous impact.

First, I realized that what I had really needed above all else was to be able to take a step back from the work that I was doing and reflect on it. Second, a sense of my vocation began to emerge, and I came to the realization that I had more to give in ministry. The decision to return to ministry was made – not alone this time – and I felt a great sense of relief as a clarity of vision was forming. I knew that I could not return to ministry as I had left.

During my time out, I had applied for a supervision course in London, but with the decision to return to ministry I sought out something in Ireland. I found myself starting the Ministry of Supervision Course at the Milltown Institute in September 2005. The course in Milltown laid an emphasis on the spirituality of supervision, and I have no doubt the Spirit of God was guiding me into the right place at the right time. This conjunction of supervision and spirituality might be a cause of confusion for some who would see supervision as similar to spiritual direction. Indeed it is, and the supervisor must always be careful to hold the boundary between the two.

In my reflection in London, I had been looking at more than just my spiritual life: it was a much wider reflection, recognizing that as a priest, prayer and spirituality ought to have been at the centre of my life. Since completing the course, I have been working as a supervisor, as well as working in a parish, and have been in constant regular supervision for my work both as priest and supervisor.

To return to the Pohly definition, what supervision has meant for me is that I have a space for reflection, for owning my decisions and developed a framework of accountability for my ministry. It is the growth of a 'super–vision' structure to reflect on my life and work. As a priest, this means that I am paying attention to my competence as a pastoral minister: I do not get it right all the time, but I am growing in self-awareness and avoiding the stresses of saying 'yes' all the time. In providing this space for others in my work as a supervisor, I hope that I am helping to provide a structure or framework for them to do as I have done, but without prescribing the outcome. It is part of the joy of the ministry of supervision to see growth taking place in the supervisee and knowing that this growth has occurred not because of my knowledge (or lack of it) but because of their growth in self-knowledge and awareness through, among other things, the supervisory process.

A theological foundation for supervision

For anyone engaged in pastoral work, there must be a theological foundation, and Pohly attends to this in his definition. The challenge for all of us is to understand what we mean by theology and to integrate it into our developing sense of ministry. Supervision can be a space where we can reflect on our understanding of how that integration takes place. This is where many would see the ministry of supervision as being the art of theological reflection – and as Regina Coll points out, theological reflection is not 'just an intellectual exercise for the sheer delight of playing with interesting ideas. Its aim is not only religious insight but insightful religious action.'[3]

Theological reflection, then, connects both the faith tradition and the practice. Because our practice of theology will take place in community – whether that community is one other person or a whole parish – our theological reflection cannot be a solitary experience.

The key to theological reflection is the Scriptures. The creation story in Genesis – our first encounter with God – calls us to live responsibly with regard for our environment in the story of Adam and Eve, and for one another in the story of Cain and Abel. In the light of these texts, theological reflection would provide a basis

3 R. Coll, 1995, *Supervision of Ministry Students*, Collegeville, MN: Liturgical Press, p. 98.

for me to situate my theological response to living responsibly in my world. I would suggest that the focus of the ministry of supervision is reflection on how we work as ministers in whatever setting we are in, in the light of faith and of Scripture.

If the ministry of supervision has this scriptural basis, we can see in the human person, Jesus, the supreme model of supervisor. People engaged in pastoral ministry talk a lot about Jesus as our model for priesthood and for ministry. Pohly presents the image of Jesus the supervisor under a number of headings, which include:

- the engaging in ministry of people
- sharing with the group of disciples
- maintaining intimacy and distance with the disciples
- challenging and instructing them.

In Luke 9 Jesus calls the Twelve together and sends them out. When they return, they give him an account of what they have done. He then takes them away, so that they can be by themselves. We see here a model of supervision in action/reflection. In Matthew 15, Jesus says that he has only been sent to the lost sheep of the House of Israel; but his final command to the apostles in chapter 28 is to make disciples of all the nations. This is a great example of the transforming power of supervision.

The ministry of supervision is also incarnational in that it has the potential to bring about the emergence of a new identity for the supervisee: it enables the supervisee to own his or her identity as pastoral minister. Certainly, this has been my experience of supervision as a supervisee. The priest who was running around doing lots of things but without reflection no longer exists. A more reflective human being is in his place. Although still busy in a parish, I have a greater joy in ministry than ever before; still not getting it all right, but very aware of that, and open to continuing learning and formation. By its very nature as a ministry exercised between people, it also develops the sense of accountability.

The process of theological reflection within supervision will enable those engaged in the process to come to a fuller understanding of their theological response to the world and the theological framework in which they operate. And just as supervision does not prescribe the outcome, so too the art of theological reflection is the enabling of the response to be made, not presuming the nature of that response.

Where do we go from here?

In practice, it is sad to reflect that the ministry of supervision is not being embraced widely. There is still a body of opinion that we are, as followers of a vocation, exempt from this kind of reflection. I know that there is a growing number of groups and individuals in priesthood and religious life who are in supervision. Late in 2008 I was asked by a friend and supervisor colleague Maranna Quinlivan to work with her at a supervision workshop for the Church in Wales. Maranna and Niall O'Connell OFM had previously presented a workshop. I accepted the invitation, and we have since presented a second workshop to a mixed group of clergy at the same venue in Llangasty, South Wales.

It was a humbling experience to witness a group of ministers and pastoral workers from different backgrounds, ministries and Christian denominations work through their understanding of the ministry of supervision: to see it as a ministry, and how they might use it in their lives, their parishes and pastoral placements. Supervision is part of the process of ongoing formation for newly ordained ministers in the Church in Wales, and it is seen as an integral part of the process. I have been asking myself – in supervision especially – if maybe this is what could be offered here in Ireland too.

This is but a snapshot of the ministry of supervision and its process. What I have written is my understanding of the ministry of supervision as lived out in my personal journey of life and priesthood. I have no doubt that for as many people who have experienced supervision there will be another story of supervision that is equally valid and probably very different. The dance of supervision is that these stories meet in a space, a sacred space of ministry and are respected and honoured as real human stories.

Believing Jesus to be our model for ministry, our model for supervision, creates a very high standard and one that can only be met
through a constant practice that is mindful of the way in which
Jesus exercised his ministry, always honouring the individual
human story and making it sacred with his presence.

PART THREE

Practice in Context

8

Theory into Practice: A Challenge for Supervisors in Formation for Ordained Ministry

JANE DENNISTON

This chapter arises from research done by the author into minis-terial formation within the Church of Scotland. She looked particularly at the integration of theory and practice as well as the value of practical placements and other requirements of the Church of Scotland Ministries Council for the formation of can-didates. The issues that arise and the conclusions that she draws provide food for thought for those in any of the churches who are involved in training people for ministry in contemporary society.

The churches are struggling. This is an observable fact, as the mores of society shift beneath our feet and the churches become ever more peripheral. Numbers are falling, and deeply held trad-itions are becoming irrelevant to the younger generations. In this context, how do we train and prepare our ministers to nurture the new – to take bold and prophetic steps into the future – while also equipping them to pastor those faithful and committed members who do not want to see their beloved church change?

The challenges are clear in the Church of Scotland's 2000 report, 'Ministers of the Gospel' (MG):

How is ... ministry to be understood and exercised today, in a Church that rightly affirms the ministry of the whole people of God and in a rapidly changing society that questions the relevance of [the] Gospel? And what does it mean to be ministers of the Gospel ... at a time when some are experiencing a crisis of identity and purpose in wrestling with inherited models and conflicting expectations of ordained ministry?[1]

This report was prompted by the recognition that for years we have been failing our ministers, and therefore our church, by inconsistency of training and lack of engagement with the real issues facing the church. It clearly identifies reflective practice as a significant tool to equip ministers for ministry in these challenging times: 'Those called and ordained to the ministry of Word and Sacrament ... must be reflective practitioners, collaborative leaders and formative learners' (MG, 2.4.5.3–5).

While reflective practice has been fundamental to professional training in various disciplines since the early 1980s, only recently has it been a feature of the Church of Scotland process. Nevertheless, it has become increasingly valued for its potential to enable and encourage professionals to challenge their own practice and refresh their skills in response to the pressure to manage decline while engaging in mission.

During formation in the Church of Scotland, practical placements are the forum in which academic training meets the 'coal face' of parish work. Trainees (or candidates) are encouraged and sustained by the supervisory relationship as the primary context in which reflective practice takes place. My own research suggests that this relationship is crucial in encouraging the gifts of reflection that sustain them into ministry and indicates the problems that can arise when the supervision offered is not sufficiently rigorous or supportive. A number of candidates and ministers were interviewed for the research, and where I quote from these interviews, I give a first name as the reference.

---

1 *Church of Scotland Blue Book*, 2000, Ministers of the Gospel, 2.2.2.

Recent developments in ministerial formation

Over the last fifty years a profound change has taken place in ministerial formation across all the churches. Historically, the classroom was given pre-eminence over practical experience, and study was isolated from the real-life situations which both students and members of congregations encountered. Indeed, Schleiermacher's *Brief Outline of Theological Study* characterized practical theology as the application of philosophical understanding.[2] This privileging of theoretical knowledge over lived experience led to a breakdown in the relationship between academic theology and the life of faith communities. Even when there were practical placements, David Lyall points out that 'the role of the supervisor [was] to help the student apply a predetermined theological position'.[3] This a priori theoretical approach was challenged from the 1940s onwards with the development of Clinical Pastoral Education (CPE), which recognized the value of reflection on practice as a pedagogical tool. The dialogical approach promoted by CPE encourages the continuous and contiguous development of both theory and practice, leading to the formation of ministers as described by Michael Carroll:

> [who have t]he capacity ... to lead the church to act in ways that are faithful to the Gospel and appropriate within the situation ... [Ministers] who function as reflective [practitioners and] leaders who function with authority – not in a top-down, asymmetrical fashion but in partnership with laity. (MG, 2.4.5.3.2)

Opportunities for reflective practice are embedded into the formation process in order to instil the habits of reflection that will foster resilience in ministry and sustain practitioners in a ministry that has the capacity to respond creatively to a constantly shifting paradigm. It is the process by which we encourage ministers to develop the skills required to react to a changing role in society.

---

2 See E. Farley, 1983, *Theologia: The Fragmentation and Unity of Theological Education*, Philadelphia: Fortress Press.

3 D. Lyall, 1990, 'Education and Ministerial Formation', in D. B. Forrester (ed.), *Theology and Practice*, London: Epworth Press, pp. 106–19, 107.

This is enabled through the consideration of the range of factors that affect outcomes, including the individual's agency and response, but also behavioural implications and, critically, theological assumptions. Thus, possibilities for prophetic action are identified, enabling ministers to respond more appropriately in context.

Ministerial formation – the process

Although, in theory, training equips candidates with skills of reflective practice, Kinast reminds us that 'moving from "what happened" to "what it means" is not automatic'.[4] It is crucial to enable candidates to make this journey, deepening their theology through critical reflection and praxis. A rigorous analysis of assumptions and ideology is required for learning to take place: 'Experience without reflection is not education.'[5]

Once selected, candidates for ordination in the Church of Scotland enter a programme of academic training leading to a Bachelor of Divinity degree, and there is a substantive 'conference' programme delivered by the Ministries Council, which covers areas of training not included in the academic degree. Exercises in Church Law, Bible knowledge and use and pastoral awareness are completed and assessed, and candidates meet regularly in small learning communities facilitated by a trained supervisor. These meetings (the 'Ministries Training Network' or MTN) are the opportunity for guided peer reflection and learning. Finally, there are four supervised practical placements in local churches, including fifteen months full-time probation, before being ordained into a charge.[6]

---

4 R. L. Kinast, 1996, *Let Ministry Teach: A Guide to Theological Reflection*, Collegeville, MN: Liturgical Press.

5 W. Pyle, 1995, 'Theological Reflection', in W. Pyle and M. A. Seals, (eds), *Experiencing Ministry Supervision*, Nashville, TN: Broadman and Holdman Publishers, p. 109.

6 A charge is a congregation or linkage of congregations within the Church of Scotland. Occasionally, ministers are ordained into equivalent posts, such as chaplaincy, but the vast majority of ministers will be ordained as the pastor of a charge.

It is widely acknowledged that learning that is focused, structured around appropriate goals and outlined in a contract to which student and supervisor are held accountable, is more apt to produce measurable results and development. Accordingly, at the outset of a placement candidates draw up a learning agreement with their supervisor. During the placement, they meet weekly with the supervisor for reflection and guided learning, and a final report evaluates and critiques success in reaching their identified goals. Proceeding to the next stage of training depends on reports from the university, MTN facilitator, supervisor and candidate to a panel of representatives from the Ministries Council and Presbytery. The panel also determines future training needs, setting goals and objectives for the year to come.

This preparation for ministry aims to be grounded in the reality of the parish, rather than in an historical ideal. Its goal is to equip ministers with tools for a very different role from one they may have seen modelled and support them in ministries that are pioneering, prophetic and visionary.

Theological reflection as professional development

To be effective, reflective practice needs to go beyond a model that simply asks the candidate to consider how well something went and how it could be improved. As David Walters has noted, to be a truly developmental tool reflective practice has to address more than mere function:

> We should ... be seeking to act as facilitators of learning in which the outcomes go beyond subject knowledge and reach into the promotion of deeper-level learning capacities, which are transferable to new and less predictable areas.[7]

---

7 D. Walters, 2007, 'Who do They Think They Are? Students' Perceptions of Themselves as Learners', in A. Campbell, and L. Norton (eds), *Learning, Teaching and Assessing in Higher Education: Developing Reflective Practice*, Exeter: Learning Matters, p. 58.

As Kinast suggests, 'there is a divine dimension at the origin of all experience'.[8] As theological educators have adopted reflective practice, therefore, so it has been adapted from the process described by Schön, Kolb and others into a more intentionally theological act which seeks to identify God's agency in addition to other factors. It is the forum where theological disciplines meet. Here, practice engages with our perceptions of the history and traditions of our faith, the propositions of our particular faith position and our biblical understanding. Theological reflection is developing into a discrete discipline, which is the focus for critical attention by a growing number of practical theologians.[9]

It is the nature of parish business is to be doing several contradictory and personally demanding tasks simultaneously, so ministerial formation is an appropriate arena for reflective practice as described by David Saltiel:

> [Reflective practice] engages with the messiness, the unpredictability, the uncertainty of practice, focussing not on abstract theory but on the ... real experiences of practitioners and the skills they develop as they try to make sense of these experiences.[10]

Theological reflection draws upon a diversity of skills – cognitive, relational, professional and spiritual – and it takes imagination to work across various disciplines and enable transformation in the practice of a minister. It requires time to reflect, honesty and a

---

8 Kinast, *Let Ministry Teach*, p. 20.

9 See, for example: E. Graham, H. Walton, and F. Ward, 2005, *Theological Reflection: Methods*, London: SCM Press; Kinast, *Let Ministry Teach*; S. Nash and P. Nash, 2009, *Tools for Reflective Ministry*, London: SPCK; J. Thompson with S. Pattison and R. Thompson, 2008, *SCM Studyguide: Theological Reflection*, London: SCM Press; F. Ward, 2005, *Lifelong Learning: Theological Education and Supervision*, London: SCM Press; J. D. Whitehead and E. E. Whitehead, 1995, *Method in Ministry: Theological Reflection and Christian Ministry*, Lanham, Chicago, New York, Oxford: Sheed & Ward.

10 D. Saltiel, 2010, 'Judgement, Narrative and Discourse: A Critique of Reflective Practice', in H. Bradbury, N. Frost, S. Kilminster, M. Zukas (eds), *Beyond Reflective Practice: New Approaches to Professional Lifelong Learning*, London and New York: Routledge, p. 131.

willingness to be vulnerable to re-enter a dissonant situation and consider the situation critically from a variety of perspectives not pre-eminently the candidate's own. A fruitful engagement with the process involves study, prayer and creativity.

It is often the case that candidates have a poor understanding of reflective practice prior to training. Experience also suggests that, as Lamdin and Tilley put it, candidates in training 'don't always know what they don't know'.[11] However, training increases in effectiveness as candidates gain understanding and develop a context for interpreting new discoveries and knowledge. As Jennifer Moon explains, in reflective practice meaning is constructed through lived experience, rather than distilled from wisdom imparted by didactic means.[12] An able supervisor as a reflective partner is important in facilitating the deep reading of an incident required to promote understanding and development.

It is clear from my own recent research that the emphasis on reflective practice promoted by the Board of Ministry in 2001 has begun to shape the formation process in the Church of Scotland today, as reflected by the comments of people I interviewed:

> The reflection thing ... got so drummed into us from day one ... it became part of what I started to do quite naturally ... in my theology ... which is why I think it's always a kind of shifting sands thing ... your theology it shifts because of this whole reflective process. (Anne)

Being required to step outside the comfort zone was a learning experience in what Sandra called 'those ... first-time opportunities where you just get sort of plonked into it, and it's actually the only way you can learn'. Kinast suggests that this requires the ability to 'reformulate one's theology in order to express the truth which that theology intends'.[13] A level of discomfort in a situation increases reflection and enhances learning: 'Negative situations

---

11 K. Lamdin and D. Tilley, 2007, *Supporting New Ministers in the Local Church: A Handbook*, London: SPCK, p. 24.

12 See J. Moon, 2004, *A Handbook of Reflective and Experiential Learning: Theory and Practice*, London and New York: Routledge Falmer.

13 Kinast, *Let Ministry Teach*, p. 122.

can be a very good learning curve' (Anne). In reflection on such situations, the supervisor needs to be able to be constructively critical even as appropriate support is offered, and to journey with the candidate in discovering new ways to make connections between theory and practice. Trust is necessary to be open to the reflective process:

> It's up to the individual to reflect. We can't make anybody else reflect; they must do it for themselves, and do it in the security that they can express themselves that they won't get any reper-cussions. (Sam)

The value of reflective practice is not obvious to everyone, how-ever: 'If you're being asked to reflect on things that you didn't think were important to your view of ministry, then ... you ques-tion the viability of that' (Derek). Courses that prioritize reflection as part of a theology degree are not always popular with candi-dates for ministry. Jennifer Moon found that 'not all learners find reflection easy when it is introduced as a specific requirement'.[14] When MTN was introduced into the Church of Scotland training, it was initially met with high anxiety and resistance. Journaling remains the least popular aspect, as exemplified by two of my interviewees: 'I still have an ambivalent relationship with journal-ing' (Louise); 'Reading back was good to see how my confidence had grown but even so I did not enjoy this aspect at all' (John).

Important questions also arise when it comes to assessing reflect-ive practice as a skill. Assessing reflective practice is potentially difficult; it can shape the nature of the learning, and there are problems about how such a personal activity can be assessed.[15] Hewitt and Smith, however, found that students are 'better able to develop their own assessment skills when they experience placements in which assessment [is] ongoing'.[16]

14 Moon, *Handbook*, p. 134.

15 See S. Schutz, 2008, 'Assessing and evaluating reflection', in C. Bulman and S. Schutz (eds), *Reflective Practice in Nursing*, 4th edn, Oxford: Blackwell, pp. 55–80.

16 D. Hewitt and D. Smith, 2007, 'Formative Assessment of the Practice-Based Element of Degree Work', in Campbell and Norton (eds), *Learning, Teaching and Assessing in Higher Education*, p. 107.

Supervision as a pedagogical process

An academic degree bearing little relation to the real work of ministry can be dangerous without practical formation, and this too was borne out in my research: 'I would say the vast majority of what I studied at university had nothing at all to do with becoming a minister' (Sandra). A high degree of responsibility is placed on the supervisor, then, to allow, encourage and facilitate the integration of theory and practice. This also has its risks, as Farley suggests:

> The alienation between theological studies and the needs and tasks of the church's leadership is promoted, not reduced, by the functionalist attempt to make the tasks of ministry themselves the criteria, subject matter and the end of theological study.[17]

Such an approach confines theological disciplines within the constraints of a didactic exercise, failing to consider the teleological and redemptive nature of the community they seek to serve. It is essential, therefore, to give candidates theological and practical tools to exercise a ministry that takes that community seriously.

While practical placements are generally highly rated by the candidates it is clear from their lived experience that the learning process is extremely dependent on the quality of supervision. Experiences range from those where 'my first placement didn't really prepare me for ministry at all' (Peter), to those where the candidate gets a real feel for ministry, and the supervisor is prepared to 'take the back off the television set and let you see how it works' (Sandra). A supervisor's willingness to show vulnerability is a significant teaching tool. However, while there are supervisors who model this – 'I learned a lot I suspect because I was used by my supervisor as a sounding board' (Fran) – others act protectively, shielding their candidates from difficult or contentious experiences. It is not always clear, however, whether they are

---

17 Farley, *Theologia*, p. 127.

protecting the candidate or themselves, and such protectiveness is counterproductive to a good learning experience:

> I think [my] supervisors ... found it difficult to admit when they had difficulties, and I don't actually think I saw a crisis situation ... and so when I came into it in my own church I found that really difficult to deal with. (Julie)

Issues in supervision

An identified weakness in some current supervision is that supervisors have not themselves been trained under a reflective model and may not have developed the skills to engage in helpful critical reflection with their candidates. Supervisors inevitably tend to model a ministry in which they themselves were trained, rather than encourage styles of ministry for a new context, as described by Peter: 'In these placements ... my supervisors ... were training me to do what they had been trained to do'. The training of supervisors in reflective practice and in what is expected of a supervisor is key to dealing with this issue.

Rigorous supervision is crucial to enabling theological reflection to provide a bridge between theory and practice: 'The most important skills [of the supervisor] are the willingness and ability to nurture and challenge the candidate's ... progress towards deeper spirituality, and biblical and theological reflection on reported ministry events.'[18] Reflective practice requires action, demanding that renewed understanding be put into practice and further tested. This means that supervision needs to be a place of safety where discomfort can be aired, new courses of action identified and risks taken in the context of support offered.

Ministry experience is not, however, simply a matter of conversations between minister, or candidate, and parishioner: the course of the conversation is also influenced by unspoken factors

---

18 W. C. Jackson, 1995, 'An Introduction to Field Education', in Pyle and Seals (eds), *Experiencing Ministry Supervision*, p. 11.

such as emotions, assumptions, issues of power and the environment. The supervisor–candidate relationship is an unequal one, and participants must be alert to this. Reflective thinking must take into account the subliminal forces of power. Support and challenge are both necessary in mentoring, but at the right level: too much support and too little challenge communicates that there is no need for growth and development, while the reverse can be demoralizing.

We cannot ignore issues of psychology and personality in the supervisory relationship, and there are many rocks on which the relationship may founder.[19] Candidates may become dependent upon the supervisor or play games, for example comparing one supervisor with another or playing academic demands off against the placement demands. Boundary issues can be significant and it is not always clear when the candidate–supervisor relationship is compromised by becoming, for example, too pastoral in nature, or too friendly. Transference, resistance to learning and clashes between supervisor and candidate are all dangers of which supervisors need to be aware. Foskett and Lyall demonstrate the necessity for a supervisor's self-awareness: the critical ability to reflect on personal responses to the candidate's experience and reflection without prejudicing the supervisory relationship. However, the ability to confront and challenge must go hand in hand with support in order to promote growth and development. Specific and practical feedback is essential and should interact continuously with the other aspects of teaching:

Feedback should motivate learners to move forward into their next episodes of *learning by doing*, and focus their efforts ... towards bringing the experience from their past work to bear on making their next work better.[20]

---

19 For a detailed discussion, see J. Foskett and D. Lyall, 1988, *Helping the Helpers: Supervision and Pastoral Care*, London: SPCK.

20 P. Race, 2005, *Making Learning Happen: A Guide for Post-Compulsory Education*, London: Sage, p. 95; emphasis in the original.

It is also the case that individuals can be closed to learning for a variety of reasons. It seems unlikely that anyone would volunteer that they are resistant to learning, particularly in an environment where openness to learning is valued. However, some candidates I interviewed identified this characteristic in their peers:

> I think there are people who come into ministry older but think they're virtually formed [who] think 'I've been saying prayers in the church I belonged to for years'. Or 'I'm already an elder so why should I do all this?' (Peter)

Learning is, of course, less likely to take place where the learner has no context for it, or does not understand why it is required: 'because I hadn't really seen how you do it I couldn't learn how to do it because I didn't know what I was supposed to do' (Anne); 'I would find it much easier coming to something ... knowing why I'm being taken through things, what I then make of it is up to me ... if there is seen to be context.' (Derek)

In this situation, therefore, the supervisor has a responsibility to promote conditions for learning, making clear what learning is expected, and why – selling the need for learning to the candidate. It is helpful, therefore, if supervisors are given some understanding of issues such as learning styles, personality types and conflict-management preferences. These tools both enhance self-awareness and enable a greater understanding of how candidates differ in their approach to learning.

Wingate observes that one quarter of students engage fully with the process, absorbing the learning and making it their own while one quarter are unaltered and unaffected by it. The remaining half *can* be engaged and the imperative on the process is to facilitate this.[21] Supervisors need to be assessed: supervision requires specific skills which not all possess, and it is necessary to provide tools and training to enable robust mentoring of candidates. For candidates, early and continuing induction into expectations and skills greatly enhance the learning experience.

---

21 A. Wingate, 1999, *Does Theological Education Make a Difference?*, Geneva: WCC Publications.

Conclusions

It is undoubtedly the case that 'those who have charge of the preparation of people for ministry ... have extraordinary responsibilities and marvellous opportunities'.[22] It is a privilege to nurture a vocation. Equally, however, there is a responsibility to ensure that the process is both as rigorous and as enabling as possible.

Four overarching themes are central to a good and helpful learning experience in ministerial formation:

- context
- reflection
- trust
- respect.

Without a comprehensible context, experience delivers little in the way of learning: 'I think I got more out of the post-ordination conferences, because by that point I knew I what wanted to know' (Anne). To learn from an experience, there has to be an element of sense-making: 'when you're just told to do it by rote, there's no context for what you are doing' (Peter). Reflection has a significant role to play in this, but a level of trust in the process and the people, and a sense of mutual respect between candidate and supervisor, enhances the learning process. This cannot be prescribed, but enabling candidates to have an element of choice in where they go on their placements, and therefore who their supervisor is, helps to create favourable conditions for respect to grow.

While academic theory, that is, theology, is not in itself geared towards the development of ministry skills, it is nevertheless a necessary foundation for ministry. However, making the links between one and the other can be difficult for the candidate, especially those who are not naturally reflective. This gap in training between experience and theology is expressed by both candidates in training and ministers in the early stages of ministry: 'The academic training wasn't vocational at all ... I was very

---

22 K. Wilson, 2008, 'Professional, Purposeful, Ecclesial and Liturgical', in A. Shier-Jones (ed.), *The Making of Ministry*, Peterborough: Epworth, p. 113.

disappointed ... ever since then I've been convinced that doing ... a purely academic degree, is not the way that we should be doing ministerial formation' (Sandra).

The challenge facing the supervisor, therefore, is to enable greater integration between theory and the reality of practice, creating the conditions for learning by enlisting the cooperation of the candidate in his or her own development. Ultimately, practical placements are the most useful context for making those significant links between practice and theory. It is here that the candidate is exposed to the reality of the parish; here that theology is challenged by the messiness of real-life situations; here that practical skills are practised and honed; here that support and challenge combine to train and equip our ministers for their own distinctive ministry. The supervisor is reflective partner, teacher, coach and mentor through all of this, and in a ministry formation programme has the single most important role in equipping the ministers of the future for this most exciting but demanding of roles, the ministry of the church.

Pithead Time for Pastors:
Training in Pastoral Supervision

MARGARET BAZELY AND RUTH LAYZELL

'*British miners in the 1920s fought for what was termed 'pit-head' time – the right to wash off the grime of the work in the boss's time, rather than take it home with them. Supervision is the equivalent for those who work at the coalface of personal distress, disease and fragmentation.*'[1]

This chapter includes comments from people who have taken part in the training described.

Background: who are we?

A Methodist comprehensive school teacher and a Baptist social worker, each married to an Anglican priest, we have both spent much of our adult lives drawn to the 'coalface of personal distress, disease and fragmentation'. As non-conformists imported into an Anglican culture, we have perhaps been predisposed not to take things for granted, to question assumptions, to try to get inside what is going on, challenging and being challenged by the context in which we find ourselves. And as dwellers now in the borderland of pastoral counselling and pastoral theology, we can feel the cold shoulder of exile both in the world of counselling and psychotherapy (because of our foolish aberration of believing in God) and in the Church (because of our kinship with the

---

1 P. Hawkins and R. Shohet, 2012, *Supervision in the Helping Professions*, 4th edn, Maidenhead: Open University Press, p. 63.

devil of the secular social sciences). This makes us not only non-conformists, but also boundary dwellers inclined to hold open the space between the two worlds in which we move and so perhaps to look at familiar things from a different perspective.[2] All of this is relevant background to our interest in pastoral supervision.

In addition, what we share as clergy partners of many years' standing is first-hand experience of the pressures of ministry on individual ministers and their families. Like the impossible tower of dishes vividly depicted in Billy Collins' poem,[3] we have witnessed how the minister daily piles on, like so much used crockery, experiences of birth, marriage, death, poverty, sickness, disability, presence and absence of God, faith and despair, joyous community and callous politics – with scarcely a moment to identify the constituents of the teetering stack, let alone the opportunity to reflect upon them theologically or in any other way. An exhausting way to exist, it can mean that the spiritual, personal and professional development of the minister come second to precision plate-stacking, doggedly revisiting human and theological dilemmas without a moment to examine their impact or to evaluate pastoral practice. It was no real surprise to us then, when by far the most difficult aspect of running our training in pastoral supervision was actually convening a time and place when participants could be induced to attend a taster session and interview. We both recognized the irresistible pull of 'the work', of honouring the years of faithful alertness, as if a moment's inattention might bring the whole precarious construction crashing to the ground.

Both of us, as pastoral counsellors, belong to a therapeutic culture where it is compulsory for such pressures to be addressed head on, embraced, reflected on and learned from in ways that are for the most part constructive, educative and potentially life enhanc-

---

2 H. Ward and J. Wild, 1995, *Guard the Chaos: Finding Meaning in Change*, London: Darton, Longman & Todd; J. Leach and M. Paterson, 2010, *Pastoral Supervision: A Handbook*, London: SCM Press.

3 B. Collins, 1995, 'Days', in *The Art of Drowning*, Pittsburgh, PA: University of Pittsburgh Press: 'everything is in its place but so precariously this day might be resting somehow on the one before it ... Just another Wednesday you whisper, then holding your breath, place this cup on yesterday's saucer without the slightest clink.'

ing. With clients, colleagues and our supervisory consultants we are accustomed to reflecting *theologically* upon psychological phenomena and reflecting *psychologically* upon our spiritual experience. Our fear is that in a church culture where this is not the norm, there is nowhere in which the teetering ministerial pile can be dismantled, and either the minister or those in his or her immediate orbit risk becoming the casualties of its collapse.

Suffice it to say, then, that the approach to training that emerged from many years of hammering at the coalface with concern and no little frustration was created with the intention of introducing reflective practice and supervision of that practice, as both resource and spiritual discipline for ministers, in the passionate hope that they may not only survive but also thrive in their work.

The client

The course we will describe has so far been delivered for an Anglican diocese. In response to the challenges facing the Church at the present time (such as reduced clergy numbers, the formation of teams, and the introduction of the Clergy Terms of Service Measure), its vision was to equip a number of senior parish clergy, chaplains and spiritual directors with skills in reflective practice and pastoral supervision.

Course design

We designed the Certificate in Reflective Practice to address the need to train ministers in skills of reflection that would support them in conducting appraisals, managing change, leading teams and prioritizing the tasks of ministry, and we have developed it in the light of participant and diocesan feedback. The twelve training days are delivered in six two-day blocks over nine months, the first half focusing on developing skills of reflection and the remainder on how to facilitate others. Since there are currently no national academic benchmarks for reflective practice training, we keep the focus on the practice of reflection upon ministry, using Honey's and Mumford's action/reflection cycle.[4]

We draw upon both theological and psychological understandings of the mission and ministry of both lay and ordained Christians and aim to create a learning community where participants' ministerial experience becomes the raw material for learning. This is built upon through a variety of activities, including tutor input, student-led seminars, skills exercises and theological reflection. Participants support and assess their own and each other's development, and tutors assess essays, verbatim reports and audio-taped and transcribed sessions. Assignments are practice-focused and form a portfolio of evidence of professional competence in reflective practice in pastoral settings. To ensure a good basis for participation, we stipulate that participants should have learned and practised good listening skills and have at least two separate situations (group or individual) in which they offer reflective practice.

Beginnings: becoming a learning community

Of course, all this talk of assignments and assessment can throw the most confident soul back to memories of the classroom, which has not been an unmitigated pleasure for many. As adults, some have found past appraisal processes bruising. Although ministers are hardly ever overseen by their superiors in their daily work, the absence of 'hard' outcomes from what they do can lead to wavering confidence and a certain trepidation about exposing this work to review. Perhaps this explains why talk between clergy tends either to oscillate between a trouble-free picture of ministry and a gallows humour bordering on cynicism or else lapses into silence.

Our first task as trainers, therefore, is to help form a space where truthful, non-shaming speech about participants' experience of ministry can take place. In addition, our pedagogic philosophy

---

4 P. Honey and A. Mumford, 2006, *The Learning Styles Questionnaire, 80-item version*, Maidenhead: Peter Honey Publications. The Honey and Mumford stages are: Having an experience; Reviewing the experience; Concluding from the experience; Planning the next steps.

is to enact and embody what we teach, so that activist and pragmatic learners can grasp what we mean as effectively as theorizers
and reflectors, so our engagement with the group intentionally
mirrors and models the processes of beginning, sustaining and
ending a supervisory relationship. From the first session, therefore, we work to establish an environment where participants can
begin to feel sufficiently comfortable and safe to take the risk of
sharing both the questions that arise for them in their work and
the impact of ministry upon them. As part of this, we pay careful
attention to our working alliance with the group, to the rhythm of
each day, to clear contracting and to the boundaries (beginnings
and endings) of the course.

The working alliance[5]

While we visit and evaluate a variety of models of professional
supervision during the course, we believe that until we have established a strong relational foundation, the learning in which we
hope the group will engage will not take place. This mirrors the
establishing of a relational base in supervision:

> It seems that whatever approach or method is used, in the end
> it is the quality of the relationship between supervisor and
> supervisee that determines whether supervision is effective or
> not. There needs to be a degree of warmth, trust and genuine-
> ness and respect between them in order to create a safe enough
> environment for supervision to take place.[6]

Hunt echoes the well-evidenced findings of the psychotherapeutic
world regarding the primacy of the therapeutic relationship in
promoting beneficial change. As in therapy, so in supervision
and training, the presence of the 'core conditions' of empathy,
unconditional positive regard and congruence are seen as the

---

5 P. Clarkson, 1995, *The Therapeutic Relationship in Psychoanalysis, Counselling Psychology and Psychotherapy*, London: Whurr.
6 P. Hunt, 1986, 'Supervision', *Marriage Guidance* (Spring), pp. 15–22.

inevitable precursor to change.[7] We therefore work to offer these qualities in our relating to trainees from the outset, and later in the training explore with the group the importance of developing and offering them to the supervisee. To express congruence (genuineness, authenticity, transparency) can be a serious challenge for those who operate within the complicated nexus of parochial, community and diocesan relationships, requiring finely tuned caution and discernment. Entering into the world of another with empathy and embracing their difference with unconditional acceptance takes the hard-pressed minister back to the first principles of their calling and the model of Christ.

To address the power differential that the term 'supervision' can seem to suggest, we reinforce the collegial nature of the relationship implied by the Latin origins of the word (*supervideo* – 'I see over').[8] Here both supervisor and supervisee take a variety of vantage points (such as use of pastoral skills, ethical issues, theological insights) as they 'see over' the piece of work that the supervisee has selected (see Figure 1). We emphasize that insight can come to either protagonist but that the good supervisor will promote the autonomy and intentional learning of the supervisee wherever possible.

Figure 1: Supervideo – I see over

---

7 C. Rogers, 1957, 'The Necessary and Sufficient Conditions of Therapeutic Personality Change', *Journal of Consulting Psychology* 21:2, pp. 95–103.

8 Figure adapted from G. Houston, 1990, *The Red Book of Counselling and Supervision*, London: Rochester Foundation.

Sabbath time and hospitable space

Our emphasis on the development of a learning community arises from both theological and psychological understandings. First, in setting up the experience, we very much want to reflect the hospitality of God for those who so often offer that spiritual hospitality to others. Recalling how Jesus' extraordinary encounter with the Samaritan woman arose in the context of his resting at the well, the notion of ministering from a place of rest is much on our minds at the beginning of the course. We aim to create an amenable balance between freedom and structure in a supportive setting which is warm (no heating problems!), comfortable (no stone floors or hard chairs), removed from daily parish and work life (pleasant surroundings, not an echoey church hall!) and refreshing (drinks and meals provided – no curled up sandwiches or church crockery).

Over time we settle into a familiar rhythm of worship, teaching input, skills work, meals taken together, theological reflection and reflection upon our learning process. This provides the dependable structure around an open space which we invite participants to inhabit in the hope and anticipation that it will become for them the kind of creative and playful space in which old structures can loosen enough for new learning to take place.

The rhythm of the day

A typical day's learning begins with a short facilitator-led act of worship – readings, poetry or music and prayers – on a theme related to the work for that day or reflecting liturgical rhythms. This may be brisk and invigorating, roomy and restful, or silent and pregnant with possibility. Whatever the content, it provides an implicit resource for the theological reflection that later becomes explicit.

Next comes check-in using a variety of creative methods to help participants focus inwards to find out how they feel or what they are experiencing at this particular moment and then to express this to the group. For ministers who are accustomed to keeping their own counsel or thinking first of others' needs, this can be about as welcome as having teeth extracted. We hold our line despite complaints and reluctance, with the rationale that making inner thoughts and feelings conscious can help us prevent *un*conscious contamination of our listening to others. Such a discipline also helps us each to register our current 'fitness to practice', an important principle, easily lost in ministry.

There follow two sessions per day of teaching input, shared between tutors and participants. Since supervision has a strong educative function, we see it as beneficial for each course participant to facilitate an experiential workshop for the course group around a specified topic and to receive feedback on his or her teaching style and presentation skills. This not only gives presenters an opportunity to receive informed constructive feedback on how they come across (as opposed to the 'Nice service, vicar' of the Sunday handshake) but gives their 'audience' an opportunity to practise giving feedback in this way (another skill essential to creative supervision). These student-led tutorials are a highlight of the course, exposing each to equal risk and invariably uncovering considerable gifts, knowledge and skill, not to mention quirky humour and individual presentation methods.

The after-lunch slot is dedicated to the practice of skills, beginning, in the first module, with one-to-one goldfish-bowl work with a facilitator, moving on to individual verbatim presentations, and progressing finally into group supervision, facilitated solely by course members in the later modules. Once individuals have summoned the nerve to submit to it, the goldfish-bowl work allows the group to see a practitioner at work and evaluate what they see. They begin to realize that what they all do each day is not so very different from one another and, with that, performance anxiety is gradually reduced. The intentional use of specific skills becomes a focus in games such as the coaching circle, Gilmore group or skills carousel. Feedback suggests that these sometimes hilarious and sometimes moving practical elements are much appreciated.

The final session of the day focuses on theological reflection on the themes of the day or on issues that are particular to the pastoral context and check-out gives us an opportunity, by comparing where we were at the beginning of the day and where we are now, to review the day's journey.

Contracts and covenants

While the boundaries of the course are held by the facilitators we cannot begin until the participants themselves have collaborated in providing sufficient safety and confidentiality to learn together. In our first session, after initial information-giving, we explore the differences and similarities between the concepts of contract (a counselling idea) and covenant (a theological one) in order to decide what kind of agreement we want between us. This takes some time.

Being commissioned by the diocese to train a group drawn from the same geographical area raises particular issues of confidentiality. Safeguarding the confidentiality of pastoral encounter is a trust deeply ingrained in the minister's psyche. So how can group members speak about their work contexts when this may involve talking about people whom colleagues in the group may know? And how firm are the facilitators' boundaries? Will word get back to the commissioning diocese? We hammer these issues out between us, and the group works out how to maintain the anonymity of those in their care without the necessity for secrecy, how to attend to their own needs to learn and be supported without betraying trust, and how to clarify the covenant we have with them.

Not until these issues are addressed to participants' satisfaction can they begin to trust that a safe enough space has been created within which reflection can take place. Our process within the group then becomes the springboard to consider what a covenant for pastoral supervision might need to contain, in terms of time, place, frequency, availability, confidentiality and its exceptions, cancellations and breaks, roles, responsibilities and expectations, ethical code/framework and reporting and assessing requirements. Just as for us and the group, while these working agreements can

be reviewed and adjusted, it is the creation of a safe and uninterrupted space within these firm boundaries that makes it possible
to reflect upon the work.

Sustaining: the course unfolds

Core model

The covenant between us successfully in place, we introduce what
will be the supervisory framework running through the course –
Hawkins' and Shohet's seven-eyed model.[9] We chose this model
as an extension of our supervisory philosophy of looking together
from different vantage points at the supervisee's work (see above).

We apply the model to describe how the focus in supervision
may be on the pastoral situation (the congregation, the parishioner, the PCC meeting, the youth group), on what the minister
actually does in engaging with it (in leading worship, visiting the
bereaved, chairing the meeting, facilitating a group), or on the
relationship between the minister and the other people involved
(the first three 'eyes'). Equally, however, the skilled supervisor
will have an eye to what is going on within the minister (both in
the situation described and in the room as they reflect), what is
going on within the supervisor, and what is happening in the relationship between supervisor and supervisee in the here and now
of the room (the next three 'eyes').

These aspects may well point to the unconscious or underlying
meanings of the interaction between the players in the situation,
and exploring them may bring further illumination. Finally, the
supervisor will have a seventh eye on the influence on ministry of
the context in which it takes place. To these seven vantage points,
we add an eighth, which is to try to see (notice, realize, wonder)[10]
where God might be at work in any of these perspectives. One
memorable teaching session involved sculpting this eight-eyed
approach to supervision, with one participant being delegated to

---

9 Hawkins and Shohet, *Supervision in the Helping Professions*.
10 Leach and Paterson, *Pastoral Supervision*.

represent the place of God in the process. Our particularly energetic God-figure danced an intricate path around and between each of the seven protagonists bringing some hilarity but also a moving theological perspective on God's total involvement in the process.

Curriculum strands

Alongside this model, which unfolds as the course progresses, the curriculum is designed to incorporate the five interweaving strands, which we see as essential to the development of the skills for reflection on ministerial practice (see Figure 2):

Figure 2: Strands of pastoral supervision

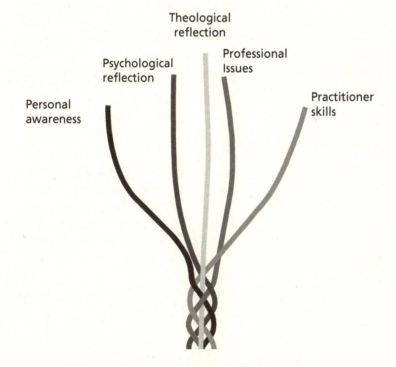

© Institute of Pastoral Counselling

- personal awareness
- psychological reflection
- professional issues
- practitioner skills
- theological reflection.

From this point on, we have included comments by course participants.

Strand 1: Personal awareness

As in any discipline that involves the use of relationship for personal or professional development, we consider personal awareness (understanding who you are and what you bring to the process) to be an essential starting point in pastoral supervision. There are opportunities to look at how far participants are able to defend or open their practice to scrutiny, to tune in to their embodied selves when listening to others, to attend to self-care and to identify the tensions and resources of their own support system.

Strand 2: Psychological reflection

Equally important is a psychological framework that can help us to unpack the processes at work in self and others, in supervisor and supervisee. Psychological models that cast light upon relational dynamics, transference and countertransference, developmental needs, family patterns or constructs such as the drama triangle are all helpful here.

The course gave me a new confidence in this area – the drama triangle was a turning point in understanding!

Strand 3: Professional issues

The professional context of the minister throws up specific organizational constraints and expectations, economic pressures, legal and ethical issues and family concerns. Here we seek to discover what relevant professional, moral and ethical frameworks can help in decision making. We examine the managerial, assessing and reporting roles of the senior minister and how these can be addressed constructively. We consider the impact of issues of diversity upon ministry and consider how, as practitioners, trainees would address questions of fitness to practise in themselves or others.

In the process of these explorations, trainees discover with massive relief how many spiritual and professional dilemmas they have in common and how much stress and isolation can be reduced by reflecting and learning together:

> I found the bond that developed between each of us was immensely supportive and has enriched my own journey of faith as well as equipping me for this ministry.

Strand 4: Practitioner skills

Reflective practice skills include both those of being a supervisee and of being a supervisor, for this is a two-way ministry. Encouraged to be in regular supervision themselves, participants as supervisees need to become skilled in selecting pastoral work to reflect upon (for example, an encounter with an individual, a sermon, a meeting, a service, a dilemma, a conflict, a celebration of work well done) and in clarifying their learning needs. They need to focus in using a simple verbal account or by employing a range of distillation tools[11] such as verbatim reports, recorded sessions, role play, creative media (for example, drawing, photographs, stones, buttons), symbol and metaphor:

---

11 See Leach and Paterson, *Pastoral Supervision*, pp. 34–5.

There was a real improvement in terms of the direction of the conversation. Questions were focused and with clear intent.

The supervisor's skills are twofold. First they must learn to provide a safe space for reflection through clear covenanting and offering the relational core conditions mentioned above. Second, they need to act as a witness and sounding board. What they see will depend upon which lens they are looking through. If they use a restorative (or supportive) lens, they may see where the supervisee is depleted or fragmented; the formative (or educative) lens shows up what learning might be needed; the normative (or managerial) lens[12] may be focused on roles, boundary issues or management of time and workload.

The course has given me tools to be able to take a more rounded approach and to use a variety of strategies.

Strand 5: Theological reflection

All of this would be interesting but academic without reference to the central strand of theological reflection. We begin by recalling the minister's personal calling and sense of vocation and review how far the setting in which they find themselves is helping them to grow and thrive in it. Evaluating a range of models of theological reflection, we go on to consider how theology, worship and Scripture form and inform reflective practice. We prompt participants to ask the questions: How do I integrate faith and pastoral practice? Where is God in my pastoral encounters? Where is God in the supervision room? What resources does my faith provide for me and those I minister to?

---

12 F. Inskipp and B. Proctor, 1993, *The Art, Craft and Tools of Counselling Supervision, Part 1: Making the Most of Supervision*, Bond, OR: Cascade Publications; A. Kadushin, 1992, *Supervision in Social Work*, 3rd edn, New York: Columbia University Press.

The training was crucial in helping us to look away from our agenda to that of the client. We were given many useful tools to aid our reflection but, more importantly, for our focus to be on God's desire for our lives rather than ourselves.

The reflective practice training has given me a deeper understanding of how to supervise, given me a confidence in what I have discovered in my faith journey and how this is relevant to the task.

Working with the group

As well as unfolding the content of the course over time, we were aware of the development of the group and the individuals within it. As time went by, we were glad to see hard-pressed ministers relax into deep sofas in break times and luxuriate in the length of a whole two days away from work. We began to see the group beginning to bear and forebear with one another and, in time, a joyful hysteria break out as participants and tutors came to trust one another, feeling our burdens shared and seeing God present in our encounters.

For both participants and trainers, such development is neither without its challenges nor does it happen without attention. As one course member commented:

This proved to be a course requiring full commitment, a willingness to persevere and to be stretched. The tutors and the material presented were of great depth and integrity. There were times when I wondered whether I had bitten off more than I could chew.

In attempting to model good practice in supervision and reflective practice, we as facilitators needed to stay alert to what was happening in us, in the trainees and in the relationships between us all.

Supervision interrupts practice. It wakes us up to what we are doing. When we are alive to what we are doing, we wake up to what is, instead of falling asleep in the comfort stories of our routines and daily practice.

Part of this was to do with not making assumptions as trainers, recapping as we started each new workshop what had gone before and mapping where we were heading in the present workshop. We tried to make explicit the links between one activity and another and the purpose of each.

We attempted to give clear information about assignments and other non-negotiable requirements, but to negotiate other elements with the group to increase as far as we could trainees' sense of ownership and autonomy. We were aware of the tension between boundaries and flexibility, and between support and challenge in fostering development. We were also alert to how absences and changes in group membership affected the group and made space to give explicit attention to these when the situation required it.

Ending: drawing the strands together

While the formation of a learning community often feels like the arduous climbing of a hill, endings often seem, like the descent on the other side, to come in a rush. Each day and each workshop had its mini ending, with review and recap, which anticipated the final ending of the course. As the last workshop approached, we invited course participants to review their own progress, give feedback to each other and critique the course as a whole for the learning and development of us as trainers. We looked ahead to the next part of their journey in terms of how they might use what they had gained in future practice, evaluating models of supervision (group, individual and peer), which they could commit to in order to keep their skill set sharp, support one another and maintain fitness to practice. We explored how to extend their learning and what support systems might be available to them, such as APSE membership, working towards accreditation as pastoral supervisors and attendance at conferences.

We summarized in our tutor evaluations the academic and professional development of each participant and discussed these and future plans with them in individual tutorials. And we invited the group – all experts in crafting rituals to manage transitions – to plan the group's ending. These have been moving (sometimes tear-jerking) acknowledgements of what has been – good, bad and indifferent – and a commitment of the future to the God who has journeyed with us.

Last words

As we look back on the experience of running a Certificate in Reflective Practice for groups of clergy and others in pastoral ministry, we recognize what a rich experience it has been. We have both relished being in a context where talk of God is expected and worship has been a natural part of the day. We have been expanded by working with and getting to know the participants who have come from a variety of settings and brought with them a wealth of experience of people and of God at work in the world. We have enjoyed watching them discover (sometimes like scales falling off their eyes) psychological keys to knotty parochial problems. We have been confirmed in our belief that reflective practice is an absolute human, theological and ethical necessity for professions whose arena is largely interpersonal. And we have shared with them the refreshment of working in beautiful, calm and nourishing surroundings.

But the course has had its challenges too. We discovered that participants needed more time than we anticipated to consolidate foundational skills of listening and responding (perhaps because these skills are given less attention in ministerial than in counselling training). More surprisingly, skills in theological reflection needed taking out and dusting off as well – perhaps, as we hinted at the outset, because the ever-increasing pile of unrelenting parish experiences rarely permits them to be exercised. Becoming increasingly aware of their own feelings and responses was also a challenge for a majority of participants, though, given permission to focus on themselves (a rare treat?), this was taken on board with relish by some.

Our learning has been to recognize that there are more steps in the process of developing advanced reflective practitioners than we had at first thought, from identifying the knowledge and skills of reflective practice, through using and practising these skills, developing self-awareness and interpersonal awareness (including awareness of unconscious processes), consolidating them through regular and ongoing practice, to facilitating the reflective practice of others. By the end of a course of the length we have offered, we consider that we have enabled participants to become effective members of a reflective practice group of their peers rather than the advanced supervisors the diocese hoped for. Nevertheless, our diocesan client has this to say:

> As the client we were looking for opportunities to enable clergy to become reflective practitioners who can improve their own practice year on year in a theologically informed manner and help others to do the same. This reflective practice course engaged clergy from a wide range of backgrounds with different skills and abilities, some of whom had not taken up many professional development opportunities in the past.

The 'proof of the pudding': does the learned practice continue (without too much process attrition) long after the course is completed? This has certainly been the case for a significant number of the participants who meet together in small 'peer-led' reflective practice groups. In addition, clergy have an increasing supervisory load as they move to taking more 'oversight' roles with larger numbers of churches. The course teaches key skills for this work and while it is more difficult to gauge the long-term outcomes it was clear that it had increased their confidence; they believed they now had the skills to deal with supervision of colleagues in ministry.

The *very* last words must go to trainees who responded, some time after the course, to a question about the impact of the training on themselves and those they have gone on to supervise:

Supervisees value being listened to, feel encouraged and affirmed and also increase their skills ...

[The course] has helped in pointing [supervisees] towards how they can take responsibility for their decisions, and conversations are a more two-way process, getting to the heart of issues.

One person who came quite anxious about what she was offering visibly relaxed as we talked through the issues she raised. [Another] person has commented that supervision is a necessary requirement as a sounding board for what they are doing.

[Supervision] allowed God to be present when we were together, enabling each of us to hear him speak and they departed feeling filled with that Presence.

Reflective practice is a crucial part of our ministry; without it we are in danger of working to our agendas instead of allowing space to make sure that our mission and ministry are directed on God.

10

Coaching and Supervision with Church Leaders: Some Similarities and Differences

DIANE CLUTTERBUCK

This chapter explores similarities and differences between coaching and supervision in work with Christian ministers. I use my own story to trace the movement from work consultant to coach, and then to coach supervisor and to pastoral supervisor in the context of ordained ministry, with particular reference to the foundational concept in coaching of a non-directive approach, and to how faith enters into the contract. The final part of the chapter discusses the relationship between coaching and pastoral supervision, which have many important features in common but are also distinct disciplines, whose differences are highlighted by the nature of the contract.

What is coaching?

The International Coach Federation gives a broad definition of coaching:[1]

Coaching is an ongoing professional relationship that helps people produce extraordinary results in their lives, careers, businesses and organizations. Through the process of coaching,

---

1 The ICF definition of coaching can be found at www.coachfederation.org/about-icf/overview/

clients deepen their learning, improve their performance and enhance their quality of life.

The word 'coach' has interesting roots. It was first used in the fifteenth century to describe a mode of transport: a vehicle drawn by horses to enable movement from one place to another. In the nineteenth century it began to be used in a sporting context about a person who worked alongside rowers at Cambridge – also to help them move from one place to another.

K. I. Tangen incorporates this second meaning of working alongside into a definition of what coaching is: 'a practice in which one person comes alongside another in order to help them achieve certain goals'.[2] The coach and client, then, travel together for a time. For me this always brings to mind the story of Jesus coming alongside the two disciples walking home to Emmaus on the day of Jesus' resurrection (Luke 24.13–35). This cannot be said to be an example of Jesus coaching but it does parallel the coaching process: drawing alongside, questioning, listening, reflecting together as the journey continues, moving towards a significant insight that inspires changed belief and action. This is the essence of coaching.

The non-directive approach

Coaching achieves its aims by using a non-directive approach. In most work situations managers encourage a culture of telling others what to do, and this is also found in the churches. It is not difficult to imagine a scenario where a pastoral worker comes to the senior minister to talk about a difficult situation in his ministry. The worker begins to tell the minister about it, the minister listens, hoping against hope that they will be able to find a solution for the problem. Once the minister has identified a solution she stops listening and tells the colleague what to do.

---

2 K. I. Tangen, 2010, 'Integrating Life Coaching and Practical Theology Without Losing Our Theological Integrity', *Journal of Biblical Perspectives in Leadership* 3:1, pp. 14–15.

In this scenario, listening is a means to telling the worker to receive a solution from his senior colleague. The senior minister does the work for him instead of enabling him to do it. This way of working is paternalistic ('Daddy knows best'), builds dependency and takes away responsibility from the worker. Responsibility for the solution is firmly with the senior minister, who has taken up the role of expert. The other person may go away not only feeling deskilled and that he has not been listened to, but also with no ownership of the solution he has been given. (Of course if things go wrong, he can blame his senior colleague because she told him what to do!)

Coaching uses many insights from Transactional Analysis (TA).[3] In TA terms this is an 'I'm OK – you are not OK' transaction between controlling parent and adaptive child. Transactions like this do not change ideas, attitudes or behaviours. They represent a directive way of working.

By contrast, a senior minister who uses a non-directive approach does not try to lead, guide or persuade. They help their junior colleague through a process with four steps:

- tell the story;
- identify what the issues are;
- decide for themselves what their needs are in this situation;
- identify what resources they have for meeting those needs and what it is possible for them to do.

The colleague does all the organizing and planning to work with the issues and resolve the situation. Central to this interaction is reflection on the actions that have led to the situation, on the situation itself and on the options available to effect a change both in themselves and in the situation. This facilitates learning and development for the worker. Moreover, if things go wrong, the worker takes responsibility and works in the same reflective way

---

3 Transactional Analysis is an integrative approach using elements from psycho-analytic, humanist and cognitive approaches. TA was first developed by Eric Berne in the late 1950s.

on what happened. Learning and development continue. In TA terms this is an 'I'm OK – you're OK' adult-to-adult transaction.

The advantages of the non-directive approach are:

- It develops reflective practice.
- It enables people to realize their potential and to identify and use the resources that are available to them.
- Personal and professional development lead to increased competence and confidence.
- It encourages self-reliance and builds self-awareness.

There are, however, limitations to working in a non-directive way and it is important to bear in mind that it does not fit every situation. For example, there may well be ethical reasons why it is sometimes important to tell someone what to do; or if a co-worker chooses goals they lack the skill or resources to achieve, the result will be a loss of confidence in themselves, in the non-directive practitioner and in the process. A great deal therefore rests on the skill of the coach in helping the co-worker to think objectively and systematically about their desired outcome and to be realistic about the availability of resources, both internal and external, to put the plan into practice.

Nevertheless, the non-directive approach is the foundation on which the coaching relationship is built.

My journey from coaching to pastoral supervision

My own journey into pastoral supervision began when I was already an ordained minister. I first learnt the work consultancy skills that are foundational to pastoral supervision with Avec, a development organization which worked with church and community workers in Catholic and Protestant churches.[4] It was

---

4 Avec was a Service Agency Church and Community Development from 1976 to 1991. It was founded and directed by the Revd Dr George Lovell. Dr Lovell pioneered the use of the non-directive approach to work consultancy for ministry and mission (not to be confused with management consultancy). A critical account

here that I discovered T. R Batten's non-directive approach to church and community development,[5] and I was taught how to apply this approach to my practice as a work consultant. The dynamic mix of the non-directive approach with powerful questions, empathetic listening and theological reflection makes work consultancy a powerful tool.

In the secular world, coaching was becoming a popular and successful intervention in the public, private and voluntary sectors, and I moved into coaching. For me, the transition to coaching in faith communities was relatively smooth. The work I did with clergy was now being informed by insights from the secular world of coaching, which embraced psychology and Transactional Analysis as well as work consultancy.

The most transformative new skill I developed as a coach was contracting (often called covenanting in the context of pastoral supervision). A good coaching contract builds trust and intimacy between coach and client and helps to create a safe space where they are able to work together with a client's agenda.

The International Coach Federation (ICF) provided me with a Code of Ethics, a clear set of coaching competencies against which my performance as a coach is measured, and a professional credential which has worldwide recognition.[6] The ethical boundary gives integrity to coaching while the ICF Competencies provide professional rigour.

It was while training as a coach that I also realized the importance of supervision. I had been one of the fortunate ministers of my generation who had been introduced to spiritual direction and work consultancy in the early years of ministry. Since I have always held myself and my ministry accountable to another person

---

of what made and marred Avec is to be found in G. Lovell, 1996, *Avec: Agency and Approach*, Avec.

5 M. and T. R. Batten, 1967, *The Non-Directive Approach in Group and Community Work*, Oxford: Oxford University Press.

6 The International Coach Federation (ICF) was founded in 1995. Its core purpose is to lead global advancement of the coaching profession. The ICF is working towards this goal by setting high standards, providing independent certification and building a worldwide network of accredited coaches. The ICF Code of Ethics and competencies can be found at: www.coachfederation.org

under God, it was a natural development to seek supervision for my coaching. A few years later I trained as a coach supervisor.

Throughout this journey, alongside executive coaching in a secular context, I have worked with people of faith, particularly ordained ministers in leadership positions in the churches, and have often seen how a coaching intervention could transform both minister and ministry. I am firmly committed to creating a coaching culture in the churches.

It was training as a coach supervisor, however, that opened my eyes to the need for supervision and supervision skills training in the churches. Supervision does not take the place of coaching, but is a parallel discipline that uses all of the coaching skills but puts them into a place where the focus is not just the work of the individual. Supervision involves a meta-perspective on the client's practice, as set out by Peter Hawkins and Robin Shohet in their 'seven-eyed model of supervision'.[7] It was clear to me that it was this meta-perspective – an understanding both of the wider context and the deeper levels of relating – that was missing in the coaching I was doing with clergy.

Faith and practice as a coach and supervisor with church leaders

Being a minister working with ministers involves implicit and explicit theological and spiritual dimensions, and raises questions about beliefs and values.

Some might say that since a coach takes up a neutral stance in the coaching relationship, they bring nothing of their own beliefs or values into the relationship. I do not believe that is humanly possible. We are all shaped by our beliefs and values. As they are part of who we are as coaches they need to be acknowledged as something that influences our work. While there has been very

---

7 See P. Hawkins and R. Shohet, 2012, *Supervision in the Helping Professions*, Maidenhead: Open University Press. For a detailed discussion of the model in a pastoral context, see J. Leach and M. Paterson, 2010, *Pastoral Supervision: A Handbook*, London: SCM Press.

little research on how spiritual or religious belief relates to the work of coaching, Bilgrave's and Deluty's research with psycho-therapists suggests a significant relationship between a therapist's religious beliefs and their therapeutic approach.[8] Similarly, Baker and Wang examined the connection between values and practice by fourteen Christian Clinical Psychologists.[9] This study demon-strates the importance of faith to the participant's sense of self and the interface between their work and their values.

It is this link between what I believe and who I am as a coach that prompts my own reflection about the interface between what I do (as a coach) and who I am (as a Christian). Taking the secular discipline of coaching into ministerial professional development involved engaging in theological reflection on what I bring to coaching as a Christian minister. As a minister I believe that I am an agent of God's love and care for people. In Scripture there is a clear and often repeated message that God knows and calls the people of his creation:

> But now thus says the LORD, he who created you, O Jacob, he who formed you, O Israel: Do not fear, for I have redeemed you; I have called you by name, you are mine. (Isa. 43.1)

God created us and desires to be in relationship with us. Psalm 139 begins by reminding us that God knows all about us: 'Such knowledge is too wonderful for me; it is so high that I cannot attain it' (Psalm 139.6). There is nowhere we can go to escape the presence of God, in space or in time, and this knowledge should not be threatening to us but a blessing. Jesus embodies this special relationship God has with us, in the incarnation, as God made man.

---

8 D. P. Bilgrave and R. H. Deluty, 1998, 'Religious Beliefs and Therapeutic Orientation of Clinical and Counselling Psychologists', *Journal for the Scientific Study of Religion* 37:2, pp. 329–49.

9 M. Bakera and M. Wang, 2004, 'Examining Connections between Values and Practice in Religiously Committed UK Clinical Psychologists', *Journal of Psychology and Theology* 32:2, pp. 126–41. See also J. Rose, 2002, *Sharing Spaces? Prayer and the Counselling Relationship*, London: Darton, Longman & Todd.

Jesus also gives a new commandment to his followers to love as God first loves us (Matt. 22.34–40). As a coach who is a Christian I seek to love my clients as I know myself to be loved by God. This leads me to want the best for them, in the same way that I believe God wants the best for me. My ministry is to create a safe space where clients can move towards becoming the people God created them to be. My role is to travel with them as they unlock their God-given potential. I believe that people can be transformed and can be agents of transformation in their work, in their organizations and in the world. These beliefs compel me to approach each client with hope and a deep conviction that they are capable of far more than they believe is possible. All of this in implicit in the coaching I do.

The faith-based nature of my work with church leaders is explicit in contracting together how we will acknowledge and draw on our faith positions, recognizing that many of our beliefs, values and Christian faith perspectives may be different. We are thus able to contract to bring the language of faith to coaching and use theological reflection as an additional tool for understanding the situations and issues they bring to coaching – or supervision.

The coaching contract

The coaching relationship is based on a contract that sets out the framework of good practice, sets goals and creates clear boundaries around the relationship. The contract is an important reference point, enabling the coach and client to check that they are doing what they have contracted to do. Contracts relate to the overall process, the individual coaching session and to the segment by segment process within a coaching session.

When a coach is hired by an organization to work with a client (for example a bishop hiring a coach to work with a clergy person), contracting has to include that relationship also. Good practice includes:

- *Transparency and clarity in the contracting phase*: The coach needs to contract with all concerned parties – the client and a representative of the hiring organization – in the same room at the same time.
- *Psychological distance*: The coach needs to ensure that an appropriate psychological distance is established between all parties. If as coach I ally myself too closely with the client, we could begin to collude against the organization. If I am too close to the organization, the client may view me as 'one of them', which will adversely affect the coaching process. If client and organization are too closely aligned, the coach may become frustrated by an inexplicable lack of movement in the client.
- *Confidentiality*: It has to be clear that the coach will not report back to the organization on the content of the coaching session. The only feedback relates to outcomes and where possible this is fed back to the organization by the client.

The coaching contract or covenant can be seen as the banks of the river within which the coaching relationship can flow. Without a well-negotiated contract the river may break its banks or dry up.

The coaching session

In each coaching session, the coach asks the client: 'What would you like to bring to coaching today?' They then clarify the particular piece of work the client wants to do in the current session and how this fits with their overall outcomes and goals. Similarly, the client's desired outcome is agreed, as well as how the client wants the coach to work with them. The client might, for example, ask for challenge, the sharing of insights or deep probing, as well as modes of working such as imagery, metaphor, body sculpting, and anything else the coach has in their toolbox.

There are times when transformation occurs simply because the client feels listened to or is able to voice, perhaps for the first time, what is troubling them. Finally, coaching must always lead to action. As the session draws to its close, the coach asks, 'What are you going to do as a result of the coaching today?' Coaching concentrates on where clients are now in relation to their work and what they are willing to do to get to where they want to be in the future. Results are a matter of the client's intentions, choices and actions.

Coaching and supervision with church leaders

Coaching and supervision both focus on the present and look to the future by planning for change and expecting transformation to happen. The two disciplines share many skills. A key feature of supervision, however, as defined by APSE, is that it is 'attentive to issues of fitness to practice, skill development, management of boundaries, professional identity and the impact of the work on all concerned'.[10] It is this area of attention that moves the task away from coaching and towards supervision.

When a church leader comes to me for coaching, we contract to work on a particular aspect of their work/ministry for a specified number of sessions, usually no more than six. We have particular goals, since coaching is more concerned with discrete tasks or projects than with the depth and breadth of the ministry itself. Areas of ministry I have worked on with church leaders through coaching include establishing a more collegial way of working as a new ministry team is being formed, managing the closure of a church, applying for a new post or preparing for an interview, working with a curate as they move to their first post of responsibility, approaching retirement to achieve a good ending and transition into a new phase of life and ministry. What these have in common is:

- The tasks are time limited.
- They are discrete pieces of work/ministry with clear goals and outcomes.

---

10 The APSE Definition of Pastoral Supervision is set out in more detail in Leach and Paterson, *Pastoral Supervision*, pp. 204–5.

- There is a clear contract for working towards those stated goals and outcomes.

Pastoral supervision moves beyond these three criteria. While using all the same skills, the scope of supervision is broader and includes specific tasks. Hawkins' and Shohet's model can be applied to working with church leaders in pastoral supervision, showing how it involves looking at a situation from several different perspectives:

- *The ministry system*: What actually happened?
- *The minister's intervention*: What did the minister do?
- *The relationship between the ministry system and the minister*: Stand outside and look at it from a different perspective. What do you notice now?
- *The minister*: What are the blocks?
- *The parallel process*: What is happening in this conversation that may illuminate the dynamic between the minister and the ministry situation?
- *The supervisor's self-reflections*: What am I wondering from my own perspective as I work with this minister on this? What is coming up for me?
- *The wider context*: the local church; organizational dynamics; stakeholders (PCC, parish, community, diocese, national church); broader theological/pastoral issues.

Most coaching is about using the first two eyes with some detached offerings from the coach's own insights into the client's work. The seven-eyed model demonstrates the broad perspective of supervision.

It is the coach/pastoral supervisor's responsibility to hold the boundary between non-directive coaching and supervision and to be clear about what is being contracted for. There are times when I re-contract with a supervisee to do some coaching around a particular piece of ministry. The contract is central to keeping the boundary between coaching and pastoral supervision clear and clean.

Conclusion

There is considerable interplay between the skills for non-directive coaching and pastoral supervision as used with church leaders. They share the same skills set and toolkit, but the scope of pastoral supervision is wider: it takes in the whole of a supervisee's ministry rather than a discrete project or situation and also involves theological reflection on the role of the minister. The difference is made absolutely clear in the contract/covenant for working drawn up between coach/client and supervisor/supervisee.

11

Therapy and Spiritual Direction:
A Case for a Generic Approach to
Supervision?

LYNETTE HARBORNE

*As someone who is both a psychotherapist and a spiritual direc-
tor, Lynette Harborne has a broad experience of both disciplines.
While acknowledging that they are quite distinct from each other,
she explores the possibility of a generic approach to supervision
that could be used cross-professionally, and argues that supervision is increasingly important in the field of spiritual direction
as part of developing a more holistic understanding of what it is
to be human.*

Introduction

My experience as both a psychotherapist and a spiritual director leads me to the conclusion that the differences between these
disciplines are far outweighed by the similarities. It is not surprising, therefore, that in considering the distinction between
spiritual direction and therapy in supervision I come to many of
the same conclusions. Nevertheless, there are some differences
that are worth attention and reflection. In order to establish some
common understanding at the outset, it will perhaps be helpful to
define the terms that will be used in this chapter.

Some definitions

What is psychotherapy?

For the purposes of this chapter we will subsume the various 'talking cure' psychological therapies, including counselling as well as psychotherapy, under one word, 'therapy'. The broad definition of psychotherapy given by the United Kingdom Council for Psychotherapy (UKCP) describes what is meant here by the word 'therapy':

> Psychotherapy involves exploring feelings, beliefs, thoughts, and relevant events, sometimes from childhood and personal history, in a structured way with someone trained to help you do it safely.[1]

The fact that beliefs are specifically included in the UKCP definition offers the possibility of a link between the processes of psychotherapy and spiritual direction.

What is spiritual direction?

The term 'spiritual direction' has perhaps unfortunate implications of a hierarchical process, and some spiritual directors object so strongly to this label that, in an attempt to move away from what might be perceived as a directive stance, they prefer to call themselves spiritual accompaniers, companions – or even spiritual guides (which for me has nuances of spiritualism and the Ouija board!). Personally, I have come to the decision that, while acknowledging that the term spiritual direction may sometimes give the wrong impression, it is still my preferred option, linking it with the tradition from the Desert Fathers through the ages and into the twenty-first century.

D. G. Benner defines spiritual direction in a way that acknowledges the groundedness of the process, suggesting that this is no

---

1 Available at www.psychotherapy.org.uk

airy-fairy business but relates directly to the individual's everyday life:

> Spiritual direction is a prayer process in which a person seeking help in cultivating a deeper personal relationship with God meets with another for prayer and conversation that is focused on increasing awareness of God in *the midst of life experiences*.[2]

That is, people seeking spiritual direction bring themselves in their entirety into direction, not just the 'God bit'.

According to Thomas Merton:

> The whole purpose of spiritual direction is to penetrate beneath the surface of man's life, to get behind the facade of conventional gestures and attitudes which he presents to the world, and to bring out his inner spiritual freedom, which is what we call the likeness of Christ in his soul.[3]

Here Merton comments on the actual process of direction, about what goes on, what happens in the sacred space co-created by director and directee.

It is the understanding of many spiritual directors that there are three persons present in that space: the director, the directee and the Holy Spirit. The idea is clear in Aelred of Rievaulx's statement: 'Here we are, you and I, and I hope a third, Christ, is in our midst.'[4] This, some would argue, is a fundamental difference between the practice of therapy and spiritual direction which they would also extend to supervision in those disciplines. The director or supervisor is seen as a channel for the Holy Spirit. For me, to distinguish in this way between the two disciplines is a little simplistic: my own view is that God is present in all things and when, as a Christian therapist, my life and work are committed to God,

---

2 D. G. Benner, 2002, *Sacred Companions: The Gift of Spiritual Friendship and Direction*, Downers Grove, IL: InterVarsity Press, p. 94, emphasis added.

3 Thomas Merton, 1960, *Spiritual Direction and Meditation*, Collegeville, MN: Liturgical Press, p. 16.

4 Aelred of Rievaulx, 1974, *Spiritual Friendship*, Kalamazoo, MI: Cistercian Publications, p. 51.

the Holy Spirit is just as present whether I am offering spiritual direction, therapy or supervision.

What is supervision?

Again, the word 'supervision' has connotations of an imbalance of power, and in this context it makes me very uncomfortable. True, a supervisor may have more training, knowledge and experience than, say, a trainee, and there may be times when it is legitimate to exercise an appropriate authority but, in the main, I prefer to see the supervision process as relational and collegial rather than one of expert and novice. It is the work that is being supervised, not the person.

The supervision of spiritual direction has been strongly influenced by experience in the health service, education and therapy. Its overarching principle in all contexts can be seen to be based on Kolb's experiential learning cycle.[5] This begins with individual experience, which gives rise to reflection resulting in the internalization and the abstract conceptualization of learning. The result of this is the final stage of active experimentation – and then the cycle starts again with reflection on personal experience.

Definitions of supervision tend to emphasize the importance of the relationship between supervisor and supervisee. For example, Hawkins and Shohet quote Hess in defining supervision as:

a quintessential interpersonal interaction with the general goal that one person, the supervisor, meets with another, the supervisee, in an effort to make the latter more effective in helping people.[6]

Many readers will be familiar with the definition provided by the Association of Pastoral Supervisors and Educators (APSE), which begins by stating that supervision is:

---

5 See D. A. Kolb, 1984, *Experiential Learning: Experience as a Source of Learning and Development*, Upper Saddle River, NJ: Prentice Hall.

6 P. Hawkins and R. Shohet, 2012, *Supervision in the Helping Professions*, 4th edn, Maidenhead: Open University Press, p. 61.

a regular, planned intentional and boundaried space in which
a practitioner skilled in supervision (the supervisor) meets
with one or more other practitioners (the supervisees) to look
together at the supervisees' practice.[7]

My experience as a supervisor of therapists, spiritual directors,
chaplains, clergy, religious, charity workers, trainees and teachers
has led me to the conclusion that, when the focus is on process
rather than content, supervision is, to a great extent, a generic
task. This is clearly demonstrated in the most influential and
developmental literature on the subject of supervision, which
describes the transferable skills required in supervision.[8]

At the moment, spiritual directors seem to pay little attention
to the theory or insights that underpin supervision of spiritual
direction. My experience as a member of a small group that
administers a list of spiritual directors in Berkshire, Buckinghamshire and Oxfordshire has highlighted that there is a wide
range of views among them about what constitutes adequate and
effective supervision. It may mean anything from an occasional
fifteen minutes for 'trouble shooting' as and when difficulties
arise, to regular monthly meetings for individual supervision in
which process as well as content can be explored. This obviously
raises questions, not only about the training of supervisors, but
also about the training of directors in the purpose and process of
supervision – and how to get the most out of it.

Context and culture

Whereas in the UK the main professional bodies require practising therapists to have ongoing supervision, in the USA this is only
expected of therapists in training. Paradoxically, the literature

---

7 For further details see the APSE website: www.pastoralsupervision.org.uk;
emphasis in the original.

8 See especially Hawkins and Shohet, *Supervision in the Helping Professions*; F.
Inskipp and B. Proctor, 2001, *The Art, Craft and Tasks of Counselling Supervision
Pt 1, Making the Most of Supervision*, 2nd edn, Twickenham: Cascade Publications.

emanating from the USA shows considerable interest in supervision for spiritual directors in contrast to the prevailing silence on the subject in the UK.[9]

While drawing on the north American literature, it is therefore important to recognize the strong cultural differences that prevail in relation to religion in general and spiritual direction in particular between the USA and the UK. In the USA there is an extensive choice of training courses in the supervision of spiritual direction, including Masters and Doctoral programmes. This is a very different picture from that in the UK, where there is no apparent consistency in the level of training programmes and no consistency in formal quality assurance. I am personally aware of a wide range of courses from as little as five days' duration to one day a week for three years.

It is also important to reflect on the context within which the supervision takes place and how this may be different from that of spiritual directors in the USA or from that of counsellors in the UK. In her book on group supervision, Brigid Proctor states: 'Group supervision always takes place within a context – and often in the context of an agency, organization or training course.'[10]

In the case of spiritual direction, supervision rarely takes place within an agency or organization – and only sometimes in a training course. The supervision of spiritual direction may on occasions be based within a theological college or seminary, and it may form part of a training programme, but each of these examples is far more likely to be found in North America than in the UK. In the UK, supervision of spiritual direction may also form part of a retreat where spiritual directors (companions) offer daily

---

9 See, for example, W. A. Barry and W. J. Connelly, 1984, *The Practice of Spiritual Direction*, New York: HarperCollins; M. Conroy, 1995, *Looking into the Well: Supervision for Spiritual Directors*, Chicago: Loyola University Press; A. W. Silver, 2003, *Trustworthy Connections: Interpersonal Issues in Spiritual Direction*, Cambridge, MA: Cowley Publications; R. Bumpus and R. B. Langer (eds), 2005, *Supervision of Spiritual Directors: Engaging in Holy Mystery*, London: Morehouse Publishing.

10 B. Proctor, 2000, *Group Supervision: A Guide to Creative Practice*, London: Sage, pp. 37–8.

direction to those wishing to engage in the process (pilgrims). This supervision may be individual, group or both depending on the circumstances, preferences and availability of those involved.

As the value and importance of supervision of spiritual direction is developing in the UK, the practice is also being influenced by the literature on supervision of pastoral care.[11] It is clear that there is a growth in the expectation that spiritual directors will seek supervision in the UK, and the benefits that it offers both to director and directee are increasingly widely accepted. In a recent survey of nearly one hundred spiritual directors based in central England, it was found that ninety per cent already had supervision arrangements firmly in place. It is both encouraging and impressive that, without any element of compulsion but rather within a climate of encouragement and education, the implementation of supervision by individuals is so high, particularly when the actual availability of supervisors at this time is also somewhat limited.

The functions and tasks of supervision

As indicated above, I would suggest that the process of supervision across professions and contexts is to a great extent generic. However, theoretical understanding of the functions of supervision is still very limited in the spiritual direction field in the UK and the necessity to draw on the literature of other disciplines is therefore even more important and relevant. The generic nature of supervision is demonstrated in the work of Inskipp and Proctor.[12] The tasks of supervision they identify – the normative, formative and restorative aspects of supervision – are as applicable to the supervision of spiritual direction as to the counselling context in which they were originally written.

To Inskipp's and Proctor's three tasks may be added:

---

11 See, for example, K. Lamdin and D. Tilley, 2007, *Supporting New Ministers in the Local Church*, London: SPCK; J. Leach and M. Paterson, 2010, *Pastoral Supervision*, London: SCM Press.

12 Inskipp and Proctor, *Art, Craft and Tasks of Counselling Supervision*.

- perspective (overview), in which the supervisor's role is to take an overview of the whole of the supervisee's work and relationships with other workers and colleagues;
- transferable elements and skills identified by Michael Carroll, writing in a counselling context;
- teaching, evaluating, creating a learning relationship, counselling, monitoring, administrative and consulting, all of which can be seen to have parallel functions in both the director/directee – supervisor/supervisee relationships.[13]

Which task is privileged in any particular session will depend on circumstances and priorities.

While the above frameworks have a significant place in the literature of supervision regarding therapy and pastoral contexts, they are still not widely known in the field of spiritual direction. Yet, these models are both simple and transferable and therefore useful when trying to conceptualize the process of supervision of spiritual direction.

Another model which indicates that a multi-disciplinary approach is a way forward is that laid out by Hawkins and Shohet in their book significantly entitled *Supervision in the Helping Professions*.[14] They consider their seven 'modes' in which supervision can be practised to be adaptable across a range of helping professions including therapy, teaching, coaching, medicine and management consultancy. These concepts also adapt well to spiritual direction and I include them in my training programme for supervisors of spiritual directors.

Ways of doing supervision

Individual supervision in person gives supervisees the opportunity to reflect on their work in some detail and for the supervisor

---

13 M. Carroll, 1996, *Counselling Supervision: Theory, Skills and Practice*, London: Cassell.

14 Hawkins and Shohet, *Supervision in the Helping Professions*, ch. 7. The model is discussed at length in Leach and Paterson, *Pastoral Supervision*.

to glean an overview of the supervisee's practice. There is also time for identifying themes and patterns that may emerge and for exploring parallel and unconscious processes. This is, however, a model that is probably more commonly found in therapy than in spiritual direction.

Since it is not always easy for a conscientious director to find a trained and experienced supervisor within practical reach, tele-phone and Skype supervision are developing among spiritual directors. With Skype, there is the benefit of visual information, which gives it an advantage over telephone. As with therapy, supervision by these means is probably more effective when the two people involved already know each other, but they may not. There may be particular challenges with these arrangements which will need addressing and working through, but I have no doubt that these can be overcome with perseverance and flexibility.

Group supervision

It is in the practice of group supervision that the differences between spiritual direction and therapy are most marked. Proctor identifies four styles of supervision group: authoritative, partici-pative, co-operative and peer.[15]

- *The authoritative group*: each person receives individual super-vision in turn and the role of the other members of the group is substantially that of observer. The underlying principles for good practice and the skills required will therefore be simi-lar to those involved in individual supervision. In this context the supervisor has to be sensitive to the individual needs and vulnerabilities of the supervisees with particular awareness of the possibility of exposure and shaming.
- *The participative group*: the supervisor takes responsibility for supervising each individual while facilitating other members of the group to take an active role as co-supervisors.

---

15 Proctor, *Group Supervision*.

- *The co-operative group*: the supervisor takes a less active role. Each supervisee identifies their needs and all members contribute to the supervision task. While this type of group is likely to consist of colleagues, the supervisor nevertheless takes ultimate responsibility for monitoring both client and supervision work in terms of legal, ethical and effective practice, maintaining boundaries and reviewing the process regularly.
- *The peer group*: all members participate equally and the leadership role may or may not be vested in one person at any one time. This type of group demonstrates the importance of members being willing to be self-monitoring and accountable as well as accountable to their peers.

When it comes to groups of spiritual directors, size and continuity are significant issues. I am aware of supervision groups of seven to nine directors, which is quite a large group for this kind of work. The fact that attendance is somewhat spasmodic in such groups is often quoted as justification for the size of the group: 'Not everyone turns up so in the end only five or so attend each time.' Further justification for such large groups is the benefit gained by hearing the experience of others: true, but there is a real danger that some people do all the presenting from which other people always benefit! A further question also arises: if the majority of those attending are relatively inexperienced, how beneficial will such a group be for a very experienced directee?

These attitudes to group supervision indicate a very different group contract from one that would be considered acceptable for therapists, where commitment to attend and to make an active contribution is expected and part of the agreement.

I admit to a slight intake of breath when I hear of spiritual directors receiving supervision from their own directors: missing an outside perspective, such an arrangement carries a high risk of collusion and avoidance of the issues that the supervisee needs to work on. I remind myself, however, of the situation that prevailed in the early days of therapy, when boundaries were very different from those of today and therapists would sometimes supervise the work of their colleagues and clients and vice versa.

There is much scope for reflection on and development of supervision for spiritual directors. The institution of universal supervision can currently only be seen as aspirational by those of us who actively promote it. Nevertheless, while current practices and circumstances may be far from ideal, and while there may be significant psychological and ethical dangers in these practices, the fact that supervision is being sought at all is something worth celebrating.

Distinctions between spiritual direction and therapy in supervision

One of the main objections to the claim that the similarities between therapy and spiritual direction far outweigh the differences centres upon the whole question of 'professionalism'. I would argue that supervision is an essential part of maintaining professional standards. Yet, there is a loud voice in the spiritual direction community that inveighs against any suggestion that spiritual direction should adopt conventions traditionally associated with the world of therapy, the mantra 'but we're not counsellors' being frequently heard. This argument seems to centre on the idea that spiritual direction is a charism, a specific gift from the Holy Spirit to be used in the service of God. However, other activities such as teaching and healing are also named as charisms (1 Cor. 12) – and no one would for a moment object to these activities being seen as professions that seek to establish and maintain high standards of practice and accountability. Supervision must be considered to be an essential part of a vocational ministry, and I find it baffling when spiritual directors seem to want to settle for something substantially less.

Another factor that influences spiritual directors seeking supervision is money: traditionally directors have not charged for their services, largely because in the past they were mainly clergy who were paid a stipend and for whom spiritual guidance was part of their role. Now that the laity is involved, it is perhaps time to review the financial situation. Training courses cost money; insurance costs money; continuing professional development costs money; travel costs money. It therefore follows that supervision costs money and if the idea of charging for spiritual direction is rejected out of hand, only clergy and well-heeled laity will be able to offer their gifts to this ministry.

The question of availability of supervisors is also relevant, as in some areas of the country it is virtually impossible to find one within reasonable travelling distance. Personally I am a strong advocate of using Skype or telephone for supervision when realistically nothing else is available, but I know that not everyone shares this enthusiasm.

As will be clear from the discussion above, I would also recommend that directors consider approaching supervisors from other disciplines. As long as the supervisor is open to working with the spiritual element, such an arrangement may be very fruitful; in particular, simply because some of the material may be new to them, this may help avoid the possibility of the supervisor making assumptions – thus giving a unique opportunity for mutual and transparent exploration. I am aware, however, that some directors would not think this was a viable mode of supervision, and it may also be necessary to have some 'consultancy' arrangement available for specific spiritual issues. Nevertheless, spiritual direction is not about abstract theology: it is about the directee's individual lived experience and their relationship with God.

Boundaries, ethical practice and supervision

The importance and relevance of supervision should not be underestimated in considering boundary issues and ethical practice in spiritual direction. While some people hold the view that the boundaries that are accepted in therapy do not necessarily relate to spiritual direction, it is perhaps exactly in this area that spiritual direction has a lot to learn from therapy. Why, if something is considered to be unhelpful, detrimental or unethical for a therapy client, should this not be the case for a spiritual directee? Equally, if supervision is considered to be essential for the ethical practice of therapy, why would this not be the same for spiritual direction? As I have stated elsewhere, I consider it an imperative to maintain the very highest ethical standards in all my work, so why should I settle for lower standards as a director than I would accept for myself as a psychotherapist?[16]

Currently, despite codes of practice produced by organizations such as Spiritual Directors International or the All Irish Spiritual Guidance Association, there is no generally accepted framework for spiritual direction in the UK.[17] Since formal training courses are relatively new and spiritual direction is still a long way from being regulated (and there are many who would advocate that this should remain the case), there are many boundary issues that are still not addressed. These include confidentiality, dual relationships, notes and records, legal issues, self-disclosure, payment, insurance, data protection and, perhaps most important of all, limits of competence and referral, all of which form part of therapy supervision. Without regular supervision being accepted as central to good practice, it is difficult to see how and where such issues can be identified, where quality can be monitored and where any accountability can be raised and explored.

Supervision of supervision

In this context, the question of supervision of supervision also arises. It is likely that, as the necessity for the supervision of spiritual direction becomes more widely accepted, the requirement for supervision of supervision will also increasingly be seen as essential. This raises questions about what training is available and it seems that courses are currently somewhat limited in terms of location, frequency and duration. However, if supervision is a generic process, as argued here, there could be much to be gained

---

16 L. Harborne, 2012, *Psychotherapy and Spiritual Direction: Two Languages, One Voice?*, London: Karnac, pp. 68–70.

17 These can be seen at their websites: All Ireland Spiritual Guidance Association: www.asgs.org; Spiritual Directors International: www.sdiworld.org

by a multi-disciplinary approach. Training programmes would be more viable in terms of numbers participating, and the element of cross-fertilization from one discipline to another could be beneficial to all concerned.

Conclusion

It would seem that the main distinction between the practice of supervision of spiritual direction and that of therapy arise in the area of expectations, and thus in the initial contract or covenant rather than in the actual process of supervision. Issues that would be considered routine by therapists, such as attendance, frequency of meeting, group size, payment, confidentiality and other boundary issues, are not always clearly addressed at the outset of the supervisory relationship with spiritual directors.

In my view, the differences between the supervision of spiritual direction and other helping professions are outweighed by the similarities, and different disciplines have much to learn from each other. At a time when a multi-disciplinary or holistic approach is being privileged in other spheres, to accept the generic nature or supervision would seem to make sense. Increasingly, spiritual directors need to be well informed on psychological matters, a requirement that has become more notable during the past few years. For me this is a welcome development of a more holistic and integrated approach to our understanding of the self and what makes us human.

My own experience confirms not only my appreciation of the support and the benefit to my practice that I gain from supervision, but also that I serve my directees infinitely better as a result. It is this conviction that underpins my commitment to raising awareness of the importance of supervision for all spiritual directors. While I recognize only too clearly that the provision of supervision of spiritual direction in the UK is not yet either well defined or wholly satisfactory, I am a great believer in Voltaire's maxim 'Don't let the best be the enemy of the good' and would therefore want to be supportive of any and every supervision arrangement that is in place. However, this does not in any way exclude the possibility that, in terms of both availability and quality, the provision can be developed and improved.

12

Healthcare Chaplaincy: From Clinical Supervision to Transformative Storytelling within the NHS

MICHAEL PATERSON

This chapter is in two parts. In the first part I explore healthcare chaplaincy as a place where stories are interwoven. The ability to stay present to the stories of patients, carers, staff and the clinical setting while at the same time attending to our own personal story and that of the spiritual tradition requires complex negotiation. While supervision and reflective practice offer ways of doing that, they are not immune to sabotage by a climate that seeks to make them normative. The second half of the chapter outlines the values-based reflective approach adopted by chaplains across Scotland in facilitating spiritual and reflective care for their multi-disciplinary colleagues.

Story-rich chaplaincy

In *Sharing the Darkness: The Spirituality of Caring*, Sheila Cassidy offers four sketches portraying the pastoral task of the healthcare professional.[1] Sketch 1 depicts a white-coated doctor and a uniformed nurse surrounded by clinical apparatus in consultation with a patient. Sketch 2 depicts a chaplain in collar and stole administering communion to the same patient. By Sketch 3

---

1 S. Cassidy, 1988, *Sharing the Darkness: The Spirituality of Caring*, London: Darton, Longman & Todd.

the doctor/chaplain has lost his female assistant, his white coat and stethoscope but still has counselling skills to offer the patient. In the fourth image, the patient/professional distinction breaks down to reveal two people meeting in the raw vulnerability of literally naked humanity. Here, where roles no longer define the relationship and words have dried up, 'deep calls to deep' (Psalm 43), and both have nowhere to hide in the encounter.

Cassidy's book and those images in particular have left a deep impression upon me and have done more to shape my self-understanding as a healthcare chaplain than any continuing professional development event or other publication since. Those four sketches taught me the difference between pastor-centred and person-centred care long before the jargon came into vogue. Sketches 1 and 2 play out each time a patient, family or staff member asks me to act representatively on behalf of the Church in prayer or sacramental action. Sketch 3 unfolds when I am entrusted with yet another story of pain and diminishment, loss and bewilderment, anger and protest. But more often than not, I am asked to simply be there, as in Sketch 4, in the silence of having nothing to say or do, mutually vulnerable, unprotected and 'not knowing'.

The life of a healthcare chaplain is a life steeped in stories: stories of expectation and promise in the birth of babies, of loss and diminishment in the face of illness, of hope and promise in transplant and reparative surgery, of gratitude and renewal in recovery of health, of grief and pain as treatment fails, of final goodbyes at deathbeds. Our role makes us privy to the public and private stories of our colleagues: a cleaner's anxiety over a grandchild, a medic's ethical dilemma, a porter's joy in getting married, a manager's excitement about imminent retirement, a nurse's marital difficulties. But more than that, we are not only recipients but also co-authors of the story of the organization within which we work: co-writers of stories about attitudes and behaviours, high aspirations and mediocre results, growing demands and lessening resources, governance and policy. And into this rich narrative mix we bring our own stories – of giftedness and inadequacy, of limited energy and undulating enthusiasm, of uncertainty about the future and discomfort with the way things are, of faith 'solid as a rock' yet 'green as a leaf'. No wonder we recognize ourselves in Cassidy's image of the naked doctor. After all, 'who else, with nothing in their hands, deals day in, day out with the crushed, the bruised and the defeated?'[2]

Yet, what I have described is only one half of the story since each time I walk through the hospice or hospital gates I carry within me another story, deeply entangled with and inextricably linked to my own. As a Christian, I carry a story of a God who sustains a world hell-bent on rejecting the order and shalom for which it was created. A God who chose to reveal himself in the messy limitations of blood and guts, joys and sorrows, friendship and betrayal, ecstasy and annihilation of a man cut down in his prime. A God who hovers over contorted hearts and minds, commitment and compromise, personal and global strategies as closely as she hovered over the waters of creation. It is in *that* story that I find myself met, received and embraced. That is the story that gets me out of bed each morning to drive to the hospice. And this is the story that enables me like the disciples on the road to Emmaus (Luke 24), to hear day in, day out 'stories of crucifixion in the unrecognized presence of resurrection'.[3]

The ability to stay present, yesterday, today and tomorrow, to stories that threaten to crush me is a professional competence and spiritual discipline not covered by the NHS Knowledge and Skills Framework. The capacity to go the extra mile and widen the tent pegs of my heart (Isa. 54.2) to offer genuine hospitality to such stories does not appear in my job description. Yet, therein lies the vocation of the healthcare chaplain. As people of faith we know the power of story in shaping identity. We, who were ourselves once slaves in Egypt, know the expectation and the reality of the land called 'Promised'. We have come through the Red Sea dryshod only to find mud and dirt on the other side. We have replaced our kings with prophets only to rail against their invec-

---

2 D. Fraser, in his opening remarks at the conference, 'Enhancing Quality and Reducing Costs: An Evidence Approach', 12 March 2012, Beardmore Hotel, Clydebank, Scotland.

3 C. Hunter, 2004, *Supervised Theological Field Education: A Resource Manual for Supervision*, Melbourne: Evangelical Theological Association, p. 47.

tives. We have hailed with Hosanna's 'one like us in all things' (Heb. 4.15) only to shout 'crucify' with the next breath. And we have become familiar with tombs, our own included, waiting for someone to roll the stone away for us. Our story has so shaped our identity that it is not simply a story. It is our autobiography.[4]

> Imagine a life without stories; those we tell to make sense of our lives, the threads we weave between us, our family and nation stories, history as story. We inhabit a world of story-telling and myth-making. Stories bear witness to our lives. In a real sense, we never get outside them. We work hard to fit what happens into them, only changing the tale when push comes to shove.[5]

Clinical supervision or courageous conversation?

In contrast with the USA, Canada and Australia, where the systematic telling of professional stories in the context of supervised training programmes (such as Clinical Pastoral Education) plays a normative role in the formation of chaplains, here in the UK supervision and reflective practice have been, until very recently, prime candidates for the 'all may, some should, none must' vote. Furthermore, where clinical supervision does feature, as in *Chaplaincy Standards 2007*, no clear definition of what is entailed or what one might expect from engaging in it is profferred.[6] As a result, models are often uncritically adopted from other professions such as counselling or social work with no attention paid to the underlying assumptions and implicit world views. In contrast to pastoral supervision, which pays attention to both the work and the worker, some forms of clinical supervision have little

4 L. Dupré, 1976, 'Memory Re-collects History into Autobiography', in *Transcendent Selfhood: The Loss and Rediscovery of the Inner Life*, New York: Seabury Press.

5 A. Parry and R. E. Doan, 1994, *Story Re-visions: Narrative Therapy in the Postmodern World*, New York: Guilford, p. 24.

6 *Standards for NHS Scotland Chaplaincy Services* (2007) adopted and reprinted by the United Kingdom Board of Healthcare Chaplains as *Standards for Healthcare Chaplaincy Services* (2009): www.ukbhc.org.uk

that is *super* or *vision*ary about them. Moreover, when super-vision takes place within the worker–line manager relationship, the lens of enquiry usually favours the interests of the organiza-tion (expressed in the focus on 'risk management, scrutiny and surveillance') to the neglect of the person who inhabits the role. As Weld notes, while quality control measures clearly strengthen the mandate for reflective practice and clinical supervision, they simultaneously threaten their integrity as a worker-centred and a learning-focused activity.[7] As a result, reflection upon practice goes in a direction described by Davys and Beddoe:

> [It] veers between line management aimed at compliance with procedures and checklists and safe surface exploration. This type of supervision becomes mundane with a 'must do' rather than 'want to do' energy and does not take up the learning opportunities that are possible. The investment in the relation-ship becomes perfunctory and tends to be corrective rather than transformative.[8]

Factors militating against transformative practice

That clinical supervision or reflective practice tend to be 'cor-rective rather than transformative'[9] is hardly surprising when we consider the range of factors that militate against them. For example, when reflecting alone, whether in the privacy of one's own head, or with a pen and journal, it is almost inevitable, no matter how self-aware we are, that blind spots and hobby horses, overestimation or underestimation of our abilities and an inability to see situations in their multi-dimensional complexity can limit clear-sightedness.

When the context for reflection extends beyond self to be shared with another or with a group, a whole host of other fac-

---

7 N. Weld, 2012, *A Practical Guide to Transformative Supervision for the Help-ing Professions: Amplifying Insight*, London: Jessica Kingsley.

8 A. Davys and L. Beddoe, 2010, *Best Practice in Professional Supervision: A Guide for the Helping Professions*, London: Jessica Kingsley, p. 81.

9 Davys and Beddoe, *Best Practice in Professional Supervision*, p. 81.

tors can come into play and implicitly or explicitly sabotage our best aspirations. We would be foolish, for example, to presume that fear is not present when people take the risk of exposing their work to each other. The person presenting their work may be fearful of:

- being judged;
- being found wanting in some way or another;
- simply not being understood in what they have brought for reflection.

Similarly group members can be fearful of:

- having nothing to say or offer in response;
- coming over as dull;
- being seen to have less insight than others in the group.

Furthermore, when reflecting with peers there may be an unconscious and implicit understanding that, when push comes to shove, maintaining friendships or protecting the ability to work together is of a higher value than honestly naming what is seen and heard, with the result that voices are silenced and eyes shaded. In such situations, safe generalizations are proffered and identification with the issue under discussion, rather than reflection in its wider sense, becomes the currency. When this happens, courage and vision make their exit and leave the door open for collusion and avoidance within the group, as identified by Mezirow:

> Any critically reflective effort we undertake can only be accomplished with the help of critical friends. We need others to serve as critical mirrors who highlight our assumptions for us and reflect them back to us in unfamiliar, surprising and disturbing ways. We also need our critical friends to provide emotional sustenance.[10]

---

10 J. Mezirow, 1981, 'A critical Theory of Adult Learning and Education', *Adult Education Quarterly* 32:3, pp. 3–24.

It is paradoxical that the current trend to promote clinical super-vision and reflective practice among healthcare chaplains itself presents a challenge to transformative practice. While that trend has led some chaplains to find in supervision the invitation to integrate personal and professional personas, inner spirituality and practical skills, others now come because they need something to put in their continuing professional development plan, or because it has become a requirement of the job or simply team policy. It takes a brave person to risk committing professional suicide by being left behind. As a result, we now see people joining reflec-tive practice or supervision groups who have little expectation or desire to reflect and minimal willingness to change their practice as a result. Notwithstanding that some people's personal histo-ries have left them with a limited capacity for new learning,[11] this 'status quo' dynamic manifests itself in participants presenting polished case studies to their peers which only serve to showcase their own ego rather than aspects of their work which illustrate uncertainty, intrigue or surprise. While low risk-taking is to be expected at the early stages of a supervisory relationship or a group's life, when it becomes the cultural norm, 'deeper learning' and transformative potential are 'left outside the door'.[12]

It has been my experience that even when all the conditions conducive to good reflection have been met – hospitality, safety, confidentiality, uninterrupted space – some chaplains simply do not have the inner spiritual or psychological resilience to engage creatively with the process. Some chaplains, for instance, seem unable to receive feedback as just that – feedback and not criti-cism – or to hear the impact the story they have told has had on other members of the group without feeling personally respon-sible or dissolving inside.

Therein lies a huge challenge. If reflective practice is to become normative rather than simply for those who are, by personal-ity or temperament, 'that way inclined', the whole question of chaplaincy training and formation in the UK urgently requires

---

11 M. Carroll, 2009, 'Supervision: Critical Reflection for Transformational Learning, Part 1', *The Clinical Supervisor* 28:2, p. 212.

12 Weld, *Practical Guide to Transformative Supervision*, p. 25.

reviewing. In contrast to the world of talking therapies in which in order to become a counsellor one has to have been a client, it is at least puzzling that someone can practise as a chaplain without ever having had to expose their soul and spirit, still less explore their sense of meaning and purpose to the loving eye of a spiritual companion. Needless to say, many chaplains do just that, but the fact that it remains optional rather than a requirement of our formation is highly questionable and impacts on the quality of spiritual care delivered and on reflective practice upon that care among the chaplaincy community.

Gifts and graces of courageous reflecting

To complement the challenges outlined above, I would like to highlight some of the gifts and graces that arise when supervision and reflective practice embrace rather than avoid risk-taking, allow courage to replace fear and engage in truth-telling rather than defensive self-protection:

- We are not alone
- Risks pay off
- Care for the carer
- Vocational renewal

Together, I believe these gifts and graces have the capacity to lead us from reflective to 'transformative' practice.

Gift 1: We are not alone

The first gift of courageous reflection is the discovery that far from being alone in our inadequacies, we are surrounded by others who also stumble and stutter around the clinical setting and become bewildered and unsure in their pastoral practice. Together, we form the wounded Body of Christ in which 'the eye cannot say to the hand I have no need of you' (1 Cor. 12.21).

The grace of telling the truth about our practice rather than hiding behind an intricate professional facade releases us from living in isolation and restores us to a community of flawed yet faithful practice. In so doing, we recognize each other not just as 'human resources' but as human beings made in the image of God. While informational learning can happen in solitude, transformational learning requires relationship:

What arises through this relationship becomes the vehicle for changing how we understand ourselves and each other. The quality of relationship is what allows us to feel safe enough to trust, to take emotional risks, to allow ourselves to be seen in our uncertainty and vulnerability, to uncover the biases and beliefs that we unconsciously use to construct our identities and ways of knowing and to see ourselves and others from fresh perspectives.[13]

Gift 2: Risks pay off

There is much truth in the saying 'if you always do what you have always done, you will always find what you have always found'. Reflective practice becomes transformative according to Sheila Ryan when it 'interrupts practice', 'disturbs stuck narratives' and 'wakes us up to what we are doing'. She continues, 'When we are alive to what we are doing, we wake up to what is, instead of falling asleep in the comfort stories of our routines and daily practice.'[14] Transformative reflection invites us into the centre of our own doubts[15] only to be met there not by the wagging finger of condemnation but, as Ryan puts it, by the respectful curiosity of wondering 'what if?'[16]

---

13 R. Shohet (ed.), 2011, *Supervision as Transformation: A Passion for Learning*, London and Philadelphia: Jessica Kingsley, p. 10.

14 S. Ryan, 2004, *Vital Practice: Stories from the Healing Arts, the Homeopathic and Supervisory Way*, Portland OR: Sea Change, p. 47.

15 E. Graham, H. Walton and F. Ward, 2005, *Theological Reflection: Methods*, London: SCM Press, p. 4.

16 Ryan, *Vital Practice*, p. 22.

Gift 3: Care for the carer

Much of what we do as chaplains takes place in noisy, public and stressful environments. Our corridor conversations are interrupted by passers-by, our bedside visits by care and drug routines, our tea breaks by pagers and our home life by on-call rotas. And yet, we live by a story which makes Sabbath rest a commandment and not just a recommendation, and love for self the twin sister of love for neighbour. Supervision and reflective practice becomes transformative when, in response to the call of Jesus to 'come away by yourself to a lonely place and rest awhile' (Mark 6.31), we 'allow, albeit briefly, the doors to shut, the noise to be reduced and a quiet space for satisfying professional conversation'.[17] In that Sabbath place, the 'rejected stone' of self-care may indeed become the 'cornerstone' that can sustain us, recharge us and propel us back into the world to face the demands of frontline practice.[18]

Gift 4: Vocational renewal

While I am conscious that our work setting is multicultural and secular, I am also convinced that supervision and reflective practice can only be transformative for people of faith if it can bring us face to face with the gap between who we say we are (vocation) and what we actually do (our practice). I worry that in turning too readily to counselling, nursing or business management for forms of reflection on practice, we chaplains, 'have forgotten our primal language' and allowed 'other languages [to] take its place'.[19]

Nevertheless, in advocating the need for a conversation not only 'on the wall' in NHS-sanctioned grammar and vocabulary but also 'behind the wall' in our native language of faith, mys-

17 Davys and Beddoe, *Best Practice in Professional Supervision*, p. 87.

18 Cf. J. C. Karl, 1998, 'Discovering Spiritual Patterns: Including Spirituality in Staff Development and the Delivery of Psychotherapy Services', *American Journal of Pastoral Counseling* 1:4, pp. 1–23. Also Weld, *Practical Guide to Transformative Supervision*, p. 130.

19 W. Brueggemann, 1991, '2 Kings 18—19: The Legitimacy of a Sectarian Hermeneutic', in *Interpretation and Obedience*, Minneapolis: Fortress Press, p. 42.

tery and prayer, what I am proposing is not some neo-orthodox withdrawal or obscurantist position but rather a theology of total immersion 'in the contingencies, complexities and ambiguities' of the healthcare context which 'seeks to do justice to [the] many contexts, levels, voices, moods, genres, systems and responsibilities' that daily face us as chaplains.[20]

When reflection breaks free from its bondage to political correctness and is expansive enough to include the whole chaplain – including his or her spiritual self – then it has the transformative capacity to recover 'that which has been inwardly sequestered, abandoned or oppressed',[21] reconnect us with the Story that underpins the work we do[22] and regenerate the 'passion [that] arises when the essence of one's life has been touched and one starts dealing with the world from that place'.[23]

Reflective practice within spiritual care and chaplaincy in Scotland[24]

Conscious that historically much of chaplaincy has been a matter for 'consenting adults in private', the Scottish chaplaincy community unanimously elected in 2011 to engage in a national programme of reflective practice in which the effect chaplains have on others could be explored.[25] In so doing it was our hope that reflective practice would meet the following objectives:

---

20 D. E. Ford with R. Muers (ed.), 2005, *The Modern Theologians*, 3rd edn, Oxford: Blackwell, p. 761.

21 N. Coombe, 2011, 'Fear and Stepping Forward Anyway', in Shohet (ed.), *Supervision as Transformation*, p. 182.

22 Weld, *Practical Guide to Transformative Supervision*, p. 115.

23 J. Encke, 2008, 'Breaking the Box: Supervision – A Challenge to Free Ourselves', in R. Shohet (ed.), 2008, *Passionate Supervision*, London: Jessica Kingsley, p. 23.

24 See M. Paterson and E. Kelly, 2013, 'Values-based Reflective Practice: A Method Developed for Healthcare Chaplains in Scotland', *Practical Theology* 6:1, pp. 51–68.

25 S. Atkins and S. Schutz, 2008, 'Developing the Skills for Reflective Practice', in C. Bulman and S. Schutz, *Reflective Practice in Nursing*, 4th edn, Oxford, Blackwell Publishing, pp. 25–54.

- to ensure that spiritual care is safe for all on the receiving end;
- to ensure that all encounters are person rather than chaplain-centred;
- to make spiritual care more effective through widening the repertoire of pastoral responses chaplains employ;
- to enable the personal and professional growth of the chaplain by providing a regular space in which to reflect on the content and processes of their work;
- to support chaplains in carrying the projections and transferences of the role;
- to provide a space for chaplains to experience vocational regeneration and renewal;
- to foster a resilient workforce and build stamina for the long haul.

The programme adopted two ways of presenting and reflecting on practice:

- the verbatim method favoured by Clinical Pastoral Education for case presentation[26]
- the 'Three levels of Seeing' (Appendix 2 and Appendix 3) for responding.[27]

The verbatim method

The wealth of material upon which chaplains might reflect is mirrored by a multiplicity of approaches to guide the reflective process. Having considered the various options open to us, for largely pragmatic reasons we settled on reflection through verbatim. While we were aware of some existing piecemeal approaches to group reflective practice across Scotland, we had

---

26 J. Foskett and D. Lyall, 1988, *Helping the Helpers: Supervision and Pastoral Care*, London, SPCK, pp. 139–42; Graham, Walton et al., *Theological Reflection: Methods*, pp. 35–9.

27 J. Leach and M. Paterson, 2010, *Pastoral Supervision: A Handbook*, London: SCM Press, pp. 36–41.

come to realize that the quality of such practice was inconsistent and often lacked focus. In proposing the verbatim method we wanted to ensure a structured, praxis-based, time-efficient, focused and rigorous framework. Furthermore, we hoped that by having a transparent published structure, everyone would know:

- the shape of the reflective time;
- what was expected of them as participants, presenters or facilitators.

By recalling a particular incident in as much detail as possible (that is, who said what, and what happened as a result), the verbatim would offer an 'as near to the real incident experience' as possible. By having someone prepare the verbatim in advance of the group meeting, time would not be wasted within the allotted session trying to elicit an issue and a willing 'presenter'. By being focused not simply on the incident recorded in the verbatim dialogue but on why the presenter had chosen to bring this situation to the group, the reflective session would 'start with the end in mind'[28] and avoid the pitfalls of either skirting round the issue or turning what should be 'reflection upon action' into more general discussion. The verbatim method was first introduced in the 1930s by Russell Dicks,[29] popularized by Anton Boisen and the Clinical Pastoral Education movement in the 1940s and modified repeatedly ever since.[30] In our adaptation of the model we identified five key questions which map the practice against the particularities of the Scottish healthcare context, as in Table 1:

28 S. Covey, 1989, *The Seven Habits of Highly Effective People*, London: Simon & Schuster.

29 R. R. Dicks, 1939, *And Ye Visited Me*, New York: Harper.

30 See verbatim format in Foskett and Lyall, 1988, *Helping the Helpers*, pp. 159–60; Leach and Paterson, *Pastoral Supervision*, pp. 73–7.

Table 1: Five key questions

Question	NHS Quality Strategy for Scotland	Values-Based Practice
What does this encounter say about my practice?	Safe? Effective?	Knowledge and Skill base Ability to be present
What does this encounter tell me about me as a person?	Person-centred?	Do I inhabit the role with integrity?
How does this encounter sit with or raise questions about my beliefs, values, world view?	Person-centred?	Dignity Compassion Whole-person care
Whose needs were met in this encounter?	Person-centred?	What was valued? Where was power? Who had a voice?
What are the implications for future practice resulting from this exploration?	Improved care experience Improved staff experience	Reflexivity Ability to translate insight into action

The third question in the table above, 'How does this encounter sit with or raise questions about my beliefs, values or world view?' merits particular comment. In traditional forms of verbatim, theological reflection is a discrete moment in the structured reflective process.[31] As such it makes explicit a correlation between the *micro* story (expressed in the verbatim) and the *macro* story of God's interaction with the world.[32] How to engage creatively those stories in dialogue depends on the stance one takes about the relationship between theology and ministry.[33]

---

31 Cf. Foskett and Lyall, *Helping the Helpers*, p. 160.

32 'The theologian feels compelled at every step to combine the disciplines that open up the past with the disciplines that help to explain the present.' J. L. Segundo, 1976, *The Liberation of Theology*, New York: Orbis, p. 8.

33 Various models are espoused, among them: (i) 'Applied Theology' which gives primacy to Scripture and applies biblical or theological approaches to practical situations; (ii) the 'Praxis model' which sees theory and practice mutually informing

Since that discussion is well aired elsewhere,[34] I will restrict myself to two general approaches to theological reflection – the thematic and the kerygmatic – before proposing a third values-based approach.

Theological reflection: the thematic approach

The thematic approach to theological reflection invites group members to listen beneath the immediate story for echoes or resonances of the great biblical themes. Thus, a Christian might listen for echoes of creation, redemption and inspiration, sin, salvation and forgiveness, exodus, pilgrimage and exile, kingdom, prophecy and renewal, passion, death and resurrection.[35]

Theological reflection: the kerygmatic approach

The kerygmatic approach considers the pastoral scenario presented in the verbatim in relation to a summary category or key story drawn from within the sacred texts. Thus, following Lyall and Farley, we could see the pastoral situation as 'a concentration of powers', situations that pose 'occasions for idolatry and redemption'.[36] Or, following the way of Ignatius of Loyola, we could seek to discern the presence of the 'enemy of our human nature'[37] who 'steals and kills and destroys' and the activity of the one who gives life in abundance.[38]

each other; (iii) 'Critical theoretic correlation' which sets insights from theology, social sciences and cultural analysis in conversation and in critique of each other; (iv) 'Critical praxis correlation' exemplified in Liberation, feminist, gay and black theology sees praxis as the determining partner in the dialogue.

34 Cf. Graham, Walton et al., *Theological Reflection: Methods*, pp. 13–14.

35 Cf. G. Loughlin, 1996, *Telling God's Story: Bible, Church and Narrative*, Cambridge: Cambridge University Press.

36 D. Lyall, 2003, 'Pastoral action and theological reflection', in D. Willows and J. Swinton (eds), 2000, *Spiritual Dimensions of Pastoral Care*, London: Jessica Kingsley, pp. 53–8.

37 St Ignatius Loyola, The Spiritual Exercises.

38 John 10.10: 'The thief comes only to steal and kill and destroy but I have come that you would have life, life in all its fullness.'

The difficulty of thematic or kerygmatic approaches to theological reflection is that contemporary human and pastoral experiences cannot and should not be uncritically shoehorned into existing normative categories. As Pattison points out, 'we need to get used to the idea that theologies can be disposable and contextual and need not be relevant at all times and in all places. Indeed they may be idiosyncratic.'[39] Furthermore, we need to be aware of making 'dubious connections which have a pious and unrealistic tenor'. It is 'much more honest', he advocates, 'to acknowledge that there are enormous gaps between some situations in the contemporary world and the religious tradition' and that theological reflection 'is as much about exploring and living with gaps as well as with similarities'.[40]

Our capacity to widen the categories of theological reflection will have direct bearing on two things. First, it will deepen our own sense of spirituality as apparently disconnected phenomena are brought into dialogue with each other. Second, it will offer a point of entry and inclusion for many of our colleagues in healthcare whose professional practice arises out of a vocational commitment to values such as compassion, care and dignity but for whom theological discourse is largely inaccessible.

In her *Scoping Review of Recent Research*, Mowat charts movements within healthcare chaplaincy that suggest an opening out from in-house language and practices to embrace the realities that lie beyond the walls. In particular, she notes the movement:

- from religious to generic spiritual caretaker;
- from responding to religious needs to responding to all spiritual needs;
- from theologically based definitions to personal definitions of spiritual need;
- from working with faith groups to working with multi-faith or no faith groups;

---

39 S. J. Pattison, 2000, 'Some Straw for the Bricks: A Basic Introduction to Theological Reflection', in J. Woodward and S. Pattison, 2000, *The Blackwell Reader in Pastoral and Practical Theology*, Oxford: Blackwell, p. 8.

40 Pattison, 'Some Straw for the Bricks', p. 5.

- from gifted amateur to healthcare professional;
- from outsider to insider;
- from intuitive-based or theory-based cleric to evidence-based healthcare practitioner;
- from organizational needs to patient needs;
- from one story to multiple stories;
- from teacher to responder;
- from outsider to leader.[41]

Moving towards a values-based approach

In my experience, theological reflection often falls flat on its face due to a narrowly restricted view of what is deemed to be theological or spiritual. And yet, when the lens is widened to include values and virtues such as hospitality, compassion and respect, which inform our attitudes and behaviours in relation to others and self, it soon becomes evident that rather than being an 'add on', theological and spiritual values permeate so much of what we do and why and how we do it. This is as true in the pastoral encounter 'then and there' as it is of the reflective group in which we are engaged 'here and now'. The care (or lack of it) which has been taken in making the physical meeting environment conducive to reflection, the hospitality with which group members were greeted upon arrival, and the inclusion of all voices and views in the reflection are all theologically and spiritually significant.

Furthermore, a values-based approach to reflection reminds us that the aim of reflective practice is 'to develop professional actions that are aligned with personal beliefs and values'[42] and that a healthcare practitioner's self-understanding is at the core of the care they deliver.[43]

41 H. Mowat, 2008, 'The Potential for Efficacy of Healthcare Chaplaincy and Spiritual Care Provision in the NHS (UK): A Scoping Review for Recent Research Commissioned by NHS (UK)', Aberdeen: Mowat Research Ltd.

42 D. Somerville and J. Keeling, 2004, 'A Practical Approach to Promote Reflective Practice within Nursing', *Nursing Times* 100:12, p. 42.

43 Based on Donald Capps' concept that a pastor's self-understanding is central to their praxis. D. Capps, 1984, *Pastoral Care and Hermeneutics*, Philadelphia: Fortress Press.

Healthcare chaplains also inhabit a world in which there is a need for them to be multilingual and inclusive – informed and shaped by theology and ecclesial tradition, yet able to converse in a manner that is both comprehensible and meaningful to the rest of the healthcare community.[44] Within a reflective space the language and method enabling participation in and facilitation of theological reflective practice can be translated into a vocabulary and conceptual framework where vocation, values, attitudes and behaviours can be explored by practitioners from a range of healthcare disciplines. In facilitating such values-based reflective activity and in 'holding' a shared interdisciplinary space, healthcare chaplains are empowering others potentially to become more vocationally fulfilled and engaged as persons and professionals.

Three levels of seeing

So far I have outlined the component features of the verbatim method for presenting material for reflection. I now turn to how group members might usefully respond. In so doing I am aware that unlike other professions such as counselling, in which group supervision is deeply embedded in the culture, many chaplains have hitherto worked unsupervised and in isolation and are not accustomed to laying their work open to the eye of the other. Conscious that group reflection 'involves high levels of commitment to the task' and 'most importantly of all, a reasonable level of trust',[45] we wanted to find a framework for responding:

- that was safe;
- that would incrementally build rather than presume trust;

---

44 For a fuller discussion of the need for healthcare chaplains to be multilingual, proficient in both the language of theology and the NHS, see E. Kelly, 2012, 'The Development of Healthcare Chaplaincy', *The Expository Times* 123:10, pp. 469–78.

45 D. Boud, 2010, 'Relocating Reflection in the Context of Practice', in H. Bradbury, N. Frost, S. Kilminster and M. Zukas (eds), 2010, *Beyond Reflective Practice: New Approaches to Professional Lifelong Learning*, Abingdon: Routledge, pp. 35–6.

- that would require a style of facilitation sensitized to the presence of fear and resistance.[46]

Prior experience warned us that without clearly agreed guidelines, group members were prone to spend the time moaning or offering advice rather than reflecting upon the issue before them. We were also minded to diminish as far as we could the possibility of chaplains with varying lengths of service using knowledge as power over each other. Finally, we wanted to discourage participants from analysing each other and 'playing the therapist' by diagnosing each other's problems, offering interpretations or prescribing solutions.

With these factors in mind, we chose to use the 'three levels of seeing' which are present in the Greek account of the Resurrection of Jesus in John 20. Since this model is explained in detail in *Pastoral Supervision: A Handbook*[47] I will offer only a brief outline here (an expanded version is offered in Appendix 2):

- The first level of seeing, *blepō*, focuses on what you see or notice – the obvious.
- The second level of seeing, *theōreō*, is concerned with the kind of seeing that arouses curiosity, makes you turn something over in your mind or wonder out loud.
- The third level of seeing, *horaō*, implies that moment when the penny drops and you realize or perceive something.

Having worked with this model for two years, chaplains report that the discipline of restricting responses to what they notice, wonder or realize has provided the safety for presenters to entrust their work to their peers, given participants a clear sense of what is expected of them and given facilitators a watching brief for holding the group. Above all it has placed insight where it belongs

---

46 Cf. Boud, 'Relocating Reflection'; Leach and Paterson, *Pastoral Supervision*; Z. Fund, 2010, 'Effects of Communities of Reflecting Peers on Student–Teacher Development – Including In-depth Case Studies', *Teachers and Teaching* 16:6, pp. 679–701.

47 Leach and Paterson, *Pastoral Supervision*, pp. 36–41.

underlying the truth that unless the person most affected perceives or gains insight, no amount of perceiving or realizing on their behalf will impact on their future practice.

The following vignette incorporates the five questions outlined in Table 1 above and offers an example of the three levels of seeing in practice.

Vignette

Mary, a full-time chaplain, presented a verbatim comprising three short visits to patients in her hospice. When asked what she hoped to gain from the exploration she identified a sense of overwhelming tiredness at the end of those visits. As the group worked through the verbatim, Paul, a member of the group, noticed (first level of seeing) that each encounter ended with Mary saying 'I'll see you later' or 'I'll pop in tomorrow'. He wondered (second level of seeing) if this was her customary way of ending a bedside visit. Linda picked up on this and said she was curious to know (second level of seeing) whether there was something particular about these three patients or about Mary herself on that day. Mary looked surprised. She had been focusing on the stilted dialogue in each encounter and on feeling unusually lost for words but hadn't reflected on the patients as a group or on how she was in herself prior to going in to visit them. She certainly hadn't noticed how she had brought each visit to a close. Jane, her part-time colleague, expressed a curiosity (second level of seeing) as to how many people died in the hospice each week. 'Too many', Mary exclaimed, and with that her eyes filled up and she buried her head in her hands. The group facilitator called for a pause in dialogue and invited Mary to take some time for herself. When after three minutes she did speak, she spoke of realizing (third level of seeing) just how worn down she was becoming by the accumulation of death after death and how on that day, worried about tests her husband was undergoing, she had been feeling particularly 'raw' and had wanted to protect herself. When another group member reminded Mary that at the beginning of the session she had wanted to explore why she felt a sense of overwhelming tiredness, Mary spoke of now 'getting it' (third level of seeing) since the personal and the professional were so closely entwined (questions 1 and 2 above). She went on to note that she had unconsciously put her own needs before those of her patients (questions 2 and 4). When asked how she now felt about the visits, Mary began to berate herself for having 'short changed' her patients (question 3). A series of attempts to rescue her by members of the group were interrupted by the group facilitator's reminder that the purpose of the meeting was reflection and not problem solving. Ascertaining that Mary had identified a way to address the interface between personal and professional realities outside of the group, the facilitator now invited group members to name the resonances that the verbatim had stirred in them. At first, group members were unable to extricate themselves from empathic generalizations along the lines of 'I've been there too'. Referring to question three, 'How does this encounter sit with my beliefs, values or world view?' Jack wondered aloud how he as a chaplain could bridge the gap between his best intentions and his actual practice. The reflective session came to an end with Paul voicing a commitment to say goodbye to patients and thus acknowledge rather than avoid the issue of death. In turn others noted what they would take into their practice as a result of the reflection.

Training for facilitators

Once the decision had been taken to roll out the reflective practice programme I have outlined across Scotland, Lead Chaplains in each health board were asked to identify reflective practice champions who would be trained as group facilitators. We quickly discovered that the first cohort of trainees needed time simply to experience the model, to become accustomed to presenting case material in a structured way and to have group facilitation modelled for them. As a result, their training was twice as long as what we currently offer.

This is largely due to the fact that succeeding cohorts of trainees now come to training with the benefit of two years' experience as a group member. As a result they know – albeit implicitly – the purpose of reflective space and how it is distinguished from line management supervision, appraisal and so on. They also know how to present case material and the parameters for responding that stay clear of advice-giving or therapy.

Training focuses on the administrative, group and reflective tasks of the facilitator, unconscious processes at work (transference, countertransference, parallel process) and group dynamics (sabotage, collusion, avoidance). It combines teaching input, demonstration, coached practice and individual learning-needs analysis. Significant attention is paid to the belief that when one person brings an issue for reflection to a group, everyone's practice benefits. Every group session therefore ends by inviting each member in turn to identify the resonances, echoes or trajectories of thought about their own practice that have been stirred by the reflective time.

Taking reflective practice beyond the chaplaincy team

As word has spread that chaplains are meeting for intentional reflection and have a simple method and toolkit for doing this, invitations have come from colleagues across the healthcare community to facilitate reflective practice for their own teams. Examples include a Multidisciplinary Team working in Forensic Psychiatry, an Intensive Care Unit, a group of Hospice Care Assistants, a Community Nursing Team, a staff-support team engaged in critical incident debriefing. A return to values-based reflection has caught the eye of colleagues across the healthcare professions and is now reflected in having colleagues from other disciplines training alongside chaplains. The training has recently undergone a process of validation conducted by a Senior Accreditation Assessor from the British Association of Counselling and Psychotherapy and has been recognized as an Introductory

Certificate by the Institute of Pastoral Supervision and Reflective Practice (www.ipsrp.org.uk).

Conclusion

Seamus Heaney describes our lives as 'a hurry through which known and strange things pass and catch the heart off guard and blow it open'.[48] When you think of what chaplains do as part of a normal working day, between arriving at the hospital or care setting and hanging up their coats when they get back home, it is not so much the discrete one-off encounters and events that 'catch the heart off guard and blow it open' as the cumulative effect of doing what they do day after day, week after week, month after month, year after year. In such circumstances, reflective practice offers chaplains an invaluable support not only to look after their own professional and personal health but also to maintain a person-centred approach that accompanies patients from the isolation to community, diminishment to strength.

When all is said and done, reflective practice offers a moment in the *present* to reflect on the *past* in response to a commitment to do better in the *future*. In so doing reflective practice reconnects chaplains with their vocational motivation and 'wakes them up to what they are doing'.[49] Chaplains who are awake to their own vocational driving force and reflexive to issues of competence, their own needs and their use of power, are well on their way to offering other-centred, creative, open, safe and effective spiritual care.

---

48 S. Heaney, 1998, *Opened Ground: Poems 1966–1996*, London: Faber & Faber, p. 444.

49 Ryan, *Vital Practice*, p. 47.

PART FOUR

The Practice of Pastoral Supervision

13

Bringing the Work Alive: A Generic Model for Pastoral Supervision

MICHAEL PATERSON

In *Pastoral Supervision: A Handbook*, I engaged in a process of foraging within the fields of counselling and social-work supervision and recycling what could be of use to pastoral supervisors.[1] I drew on the insights of Hawkins and Shohet, Inskipp and Proctor, Carroll and Lahad.[2] While I remain indebted to each of these writers for my formation and inspiration as a supervisor, I have become increasingly uneasy with the dominant therapeutic paradigm inherent in supervision and grateful to alternative voices who highlight other dimensions, including: Maureen Conroy, who underscores the contemplative character of supervision;[3] Juan Reed, who encourages 'holy looking', especially on the margins of the supervisory space;[4] Sheila Ryan, who sees supervision as a moment of reconnection with core values and motivation;[5] Nicki

---

1 J. Leach and M. Paterson, 2010, *Pastoral Supervision: A Handbook*, London: SCM Press.

2 P. Hawkins and R. Shohet, 2006, *Supervision in the Helping Professions*, 2nd edn, Maidenhead: Open University Press; F. Inskipp and B. Proctor, 1993, *The Art, Craft and Tasks of Counselling Supervision*, Twickenham: Cascade; M. Carroll and M. Tholstrup (eds), 2001, *Integrative Approaches to Supervision*, London and Philadelphia: Jessica Kingsley; M. Lahad, 2000, *Creative Supervision*, London and Philadelphia: Jessica Kingsley.

3 M. Conroy, 1995, *Looking into the Well: Supervision of Spiritual Directors*, Chicago: Loyola University Press.

4 J. Reed, 2003, 'Can I get a Witness? Spiritual Direction with the Marginalized', in N. Vest (ed.), 2000, *Still Listening*, Harrisburg, PA: Morehouse Publishing, pp. 93–104.

5 S. Ryan, 2004, *Vital Practice: Stories from the Healing Arts, the Homeopathic and Supervisory Way*, Portland, OR: Sea Change.

Weld, who brings the transformative dimension to the fore;[6] Geraldine Holton, who considers supervision as an invitation to playfulness in Wisdom's garden;[7] and Davys and Beddoe,[8] who think outside the therapeutic box.

As interest increases in supervision across disciplines outside therapy and counselling, I now propose a generic model of supervision that can be used both with individuals and with groups. I have devised it with three kinds of supervising practitioner in mind:

- those who do not have the therapeutic hinterland with which to embrace the dominant models that are currently available;
- experienced supervisors whose supervisees have little interest in the psychodynamic processes that underpin extant models;
- supervisors who wish to work cross-professionally where the ability to use generic skills and hold an intentional space is of greater value than first-hand knowledge of the particular profession or sphere of activity.

In presenting this blended model I make no claim to originality. I draw on Page and Wosket and adapt their cyclical map for the reflective session.[9] I also draw on Mogs Bazely's expansion of the John 20 'three levels of seeing' for responding to what is presented (see Appendix 2 and Appendix 3). And into the mix I add attention to hospitality, presence and wisdom, all of which are essential if supervision is to be soulful.

---

6 N. Weld, 2012, *A Practical Guide to Transformative Supervision for the Helping Professions: Amplifying Insight*, London: Jessica Kingsley.

7 M. Benefiel and G. Holton, 2011, *The Soul of Supervision: Integrating Practice and Theory*, New York: Morehouse Publishing.

8 A. Davys and L. Beddoe, 2010, *Best Practice in Professional Supervision: A Guide for the Helping Professions*, London: Jessica Kingsley.

9 S. Page and V. Wosket, 1994, *Supervising the Counsellor: A Cyclical Model*, London: Routledge.

Mapping a supervision session

As an intentional space, supervision has a clear structure characterized by six processes as outlined in Figure 1:

Figure 1: Map of supervision session

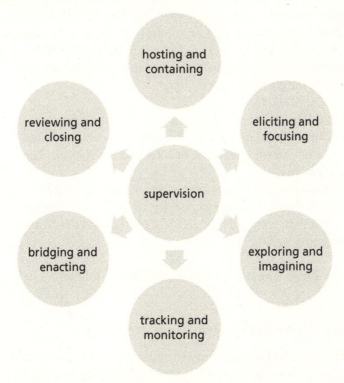

- *Hosting and containing* focuses on the kind of hospitality which enables transformative learning. This includes attention to the ethical framework, organization culture, immediate environment and quality of interpersonal relationship between participants.
- *Eliciting and focusing* is not only about getting the work into the room but about identifying the energy or impulse that will make reflection worthwhile; that is: What is it in particular about this that makes it worth looking at here today?

- *Exploring and imagining*: Once a focus has been established, exploring and imagining becomes a playful and creatively fertile place in which to try out ideas and ways of working. It is also the place in which stray thoughts, fantasies, images and metaphors can be aired.
- *Tracking and monitoring*: Tracking is both a discrete moment in the reflective cycle and something that runs through the whole session. It is a way of monitoring that what is happening is matching what it is needed within the allotted time.
- *Bridging and enacting* are reminders that we reflect on work
  - from the *past*
  - in the *present*
  - in order to change and enhance work in the *future*.
  A bridge is built out from the reflective time and back into the world of everyday practice. Enacting names the first steps to be taken.
- *Reviewing and closing* is the process of naming what has been learned through reflection and the drawing of a line on the exploration. In supervision, closing well is just as important as beginning well.

Each of the six components can be unfolded as follows.

Hosting and containing – supervision as hospitality

Hosting and containing can be summed up as attentive hospitality. If guests are coming for dinner, it would be inhospitable to have no food in the house to give them when they arrive. Similarly, if guests are vegetarian, it would be inhospitable to serve them steak. Hospitality requires anticipating what guests may need and being ready to accommodate those needs. Likewise, hospitable supervision gives central place to the supervisee and requires the supervisor to be eccentric; that is, to stand back (*ex*) from the centre (*centrum*) to make space for the other.

As supervision has developed, so has the lens of interpretation widened from understandings of it primarily as quality control (*over*-seeing) to an opportunity for ongoing transformative learning (*super*-seeing, better-*vision*). Reflecting on the *past* in the *present* in order to improve the *future* turns history into learning. As such, supervision becomes a regular place of continuing professional development where what is already known can meet with what *needs* to be known. It is a learning space.

According to Parker Palmer, learning spaces have three essential dimensions:

- openness
- boundaries and
- an air of hospitality.

Openness requires clearing away the clutter of being occupied with the past and worrying about the future to make space for the present, the 'now' of this moment. As Palmer reminds us, however, 'the openness of a space is created by the firmness of its *boundaries*'. Since supervision offers an intentional structure for learning and not what Palmer calls 'an invitation to confusion and chaos', clarity of purpose, role, use of time and expectation all need to be spelt out. Furthermore, since supervision involves an intricate dialogue between practice, practitioner and working context, this kind of learning can be challenging and unsettling. To enable supervision to remain a learning place, it requires to be conducted in an air of hospitality. According to Palmer, 'hospitality means receiving each other, our struggles, our newborn ideas, with openness and care'. Hospitable supervision 'will be a place where every stranger and every strange utterance is met with welcome'.[10]

Hosting and containing, then, has six components which will be provided by a supervisor who is attentive to hospitality, as in Figure 2:

---

10 P. J. Palmer, 1993, *To Know as We are Known: A Spirituality of Education*, San Francisco: HarperOne, pp. 71–5.

Figure 2: Hosting and containing

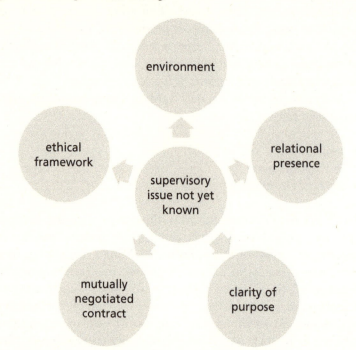

- *A physical environment conducive to reflection.* The physical environment is often neglected in the literature on supervision. This may be a reflection of the therapeutic stable from which much of it arises in which it is assumed that supervision is conducted by mature and experienced counsellors and therapists who do not need such a reminder. However, since pastoral work often takes place outwith clearly defined therapeutic frames of reference, it is worth considering basic questions such as: If I were coming to this space with something that really mattered to me, would this room help or hinder me exploring it? Are these the kind of chairs that encourage the exploration of work or a cosy chat? Is the room warm enough for a comfortable hour together? Will we be disturbed? Have intrusions been anticipated (phones switched off, 'room in use' indicated and so on)?

- *Physical, cognitive, psychological and spiritual presence.* Relational presence is of the essence in supervision. No matter how ideal the physical environment or the skill of the supervisor, supervision simply will not be possible if those involved cannot relate to each other. While supervisors cannot be held responsible for the psychological make-up of supervisees, they are ethically responsible for their own part in making room within their own hearts and minds to welcome their guests. Mindful attentiveness on the part of the supervisor prior to arrival will afford supervisees a space between past and future practice to attend to whatever is on their mind. Supervisors are truly present when they have cleared a space within their own busy heads and hearts to 'lend' themselves mentally, affectively and spiritually to the other. Without this inner spaciousness, supervisors will be unable to make intentional use of themselves and will leave their supervisees cheated. They will also model a lack of presence to supervisees – who may repeat that pattern with their clients.

- *Clarity about the purpose of the time together* is often lacking in cross-professional supervision. Since the territory and contours of supervision are still largely unknown in many disciplines, the first task of supervision is to teach people what the space is for. Those who present as supervisees need to discover whether an exploration of work and themselves within it is really what they are looking for, or if personal counselling or spiritual direction is more suited to their needs. Clarity of purpose frees supervisees to know what to bring to sessions and what to reflect on with others elsewhere. It also frees supervisors to note issues of therapeutic or spiritual significance without adopting the role of therapist or soul friend. When people of faith begin to develop, reflexivity issues pertinent to all three caring professions may emerge. Being clear about what belongs where makes for good supervisory hygiene.

- *A mutually agreed contract or covenant for the work.* The covenant or contract *for working* needs to be co-constructed. What is the supervisor responsible for? What is the supervisee responsible for? How often are they to meet? How long will meetings last? Are expectations clear about payment and how it is to be made? Is there a cancellation policy? Is there a contract for dealing with issues of fitness to practice and breaks in practice? Is the work ongoing or finite? Is review built in?

- *A framework of ethical practice underpinning everything.* The entire relationship and all the processes that serve it need to be held within an explicit ethical framework rather than a vague desire to do good and cause no harm. By what code of practice does the supervisor operate? To whom could a supervisee raise issues of concern about the supervisor? Conversely, is the supervisory contract a hermetically sealed private affair between the two parties or are there contractual or organizational factors to consider? Are reports to be written? Are there any legal implications for the work? Is the supervisor covered by professional indemnity insurance and so on?

Eliciting and focusing

Nothing does more to kill the energy in supervision than an anxious supervisor who alights on the first thing a supervisee says in a session and presumes to make that the focus for the session. Sometimes supervisees come knowing exactly what they want to talk about and what they are looking for in wanting to explore it. Sometimes they come knowing that a particular incident or encounter has 'stayed with them' and tugged at their mind or heart but cannot identify why it matters or what it relates to. And sometimes people come not knowing where to begin. This can be for a variety of reasons. Those who are new to supervision may not have the tools to sift through weeks of practice to know what to bring. Those who are overwhelmed by their work may be aware that a decision to bring one issue to supervision closes the door on a cluster of other issues and may find it difficult to know which to choose. Others again may be so detached from their work that it no longer impinges upon their mental and spiritual energies.

Figure 3 shows the essential components of eliciting and focusing:

Figure 3: Eliciting and focusing

- *What are you bringing?* The first duty of the supervisor is to teach the supervisee how to use the space called supervision within which eliciting a supervisory question or issue is paramount. The question 'What are you bringing to supervision?' can be answered in a number of ways. Often a supervisee will alight on a particular experience: 'being bored listening to someone's story', 'chairing a meeting and going blank when asked a question', 'not knowing my way around something'. At other times what supervisees bring is not so much a particular issue as an aspect of themselves in the work: 'I used to love nursing, but right now the pressure is unbearable', 'I feel at a professional crossroads', 'I have had a busy month since we last met but right now I feel blank'. When supervisees simply do not know what to bring, there are useful tools for getting the work into the room, such as six-minute journaling exercises, choosing a postcard that resonates with their current professional experience, making a small installation using objects, stones, buttons to represent their work or drawing a time line of professional highs and lows.[11]

- *Why are you bringing it here?* Wherever supervision takes place, the word 'work' is written above the door. Personal and spiritual issues do arise in supervision but need to be respectfully and reverently handled in so far as they impinge on the supervisee's ability to work effectively. There is a humility built into supervision which recognizes that it is only one form of supportive relationship with its own particular focus and set of skills. Supervisors need to protect the integrity and limitations of their role no matter how hard supervisees push them to play the therapist or spiritual guide. Nevertheless, establishing the legitimacy of an issue is only the first step in supervision. Further exploration is needed to know why someone chooses to bring an issue to supervision rather than to a line manager, work colleague or personal friend.

- *Why are you bringing it today?* The question may seem pedantic and may not always be asked in such an explicit way, but supervisors will do well to listen between the lines for hints of an answer. Is the issue urgent and requiring immediate solution? ('I am giving a talk next week about X and feel stuck.') Is the issue recurring and therefore presenting itself for exploration now? ('This was the third time that week I had told a parent that they had no idea what pressure we teachers were under.') Is the issue impeding other work from taking place? ('I can't get what has happened to L out of my mind and feel I am neglecting all the other kids in the youth club.') Asking 'Why today?' will help focus the use of time.

- *What do you want in bringing it?* A supervisee who can answer this question is well on their way to insight. 'I am looking for a second opinion that what I did was not off the wall' (supervision as validation). 'I feel ashamed about messing up at work and need to unravel the mess (supervision as catharsis). 'I feel

---

11 See Leach and Paterson, *Pastoral Supervision.*

chuffed that I managed to confront my fears for a change and speak up for myself' (supervision as bearing witness). 'I have been over this again and again in my head and even talked it through with colleagues but I fear I may be deceiving myself' (supervision as courageous conversation). People have many reasons for bringing their work to supervision, a fraction of which are voiced explicitly. Practitioners' developmental stages have a part to play in what they might be looking for. For example, a novice practitioner may be seeking direct instruction (what to do, what to say), whereas a mature practitioner may simply be looking for someone to afford them the quality of hearing that they themselves offer others (consultative support).

- *Agreeing a focus*. Agreeing a focus is an expression of hospitality. Just as a host would not give a cup of tea to a guest who had requested a beer, so too a supervisor who has elicited a focus needs to respond to that focus and not follow their own interests. In practice this means that once the supervisory issue or focus has been established, every subsequent intervention needs to be attuned to that issue. This requires discipline (the agenda is set by the supervisee and not the supervisor); repertoire (a range of ways of going deeper into the issue that has been identified) and monitoring (are we dealing with the real issue here or getting sidetracked?).

Exploring and imagining

While exploration is the very air that therapists and counsellors breathe, it comes less naturally to many others. In practice many people faced with a problem immediately begin scrambling around for a solution. While this is sometimes exactly what is required, overuse of quick-fix solutions renders exploration redundant. When it comes to supervision we are not dealing so much with problems that need to be fixed as people who need to be accompanied. This is based on the wisdom that the first authority on the client is the client. The second is the practitioner and only

Figure 4: Exploring and imagining

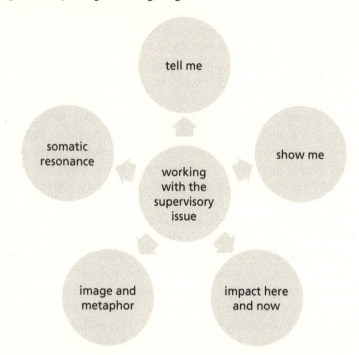

the third is the supervisor. Admittedly, supervisees do not always present themselves and their dilemmas in that way but effective supervisors do well to remember that and resist the projections to which they are regularly subjected.

Without due attention to exploration, supervision risks becoming an advice shop in which a wise all-knowing person (the supervisor) dispenses wisdom to a less experienced person (the supervisee) who is expected to be grateful. Such outdated models of supervision accentuate the power dynamic between the two parties and invite dependency and obedience rather than professional development and transformative learning. Exploration accounts for about two thirds of the time allotted for supervision. Since there is an abundance of literature on how to explore issues in supervision I shall simply note some of the key points here as shown in Figure 4.

- *Tell me.* The 'Telling' approach favours speech and cognition. Thus, a supervisor may say: 'Describe the scene for me. Who was there? Where were you in the room? Were you standing or sitting? Tell me how you were feeling before the incident occurred. Talk me through your thought processes, the inner commentary which was running in your head as the scene unfolded? Tell me your stray thoughts or fantasies about the person you were dealing with. Tell me what you would say to your client, if there were no holds barred. Tell me who she reminds you of. Tell me about other times in your life where you have had to face similar things.' Supervisors need to be attentive to the possibility that the 'tell me' approach can establish a pattern of question and answer or be experienced as forensic investigation, and need to use it only in so far as it enables exploration.

- *Show me.* 'Showing' approaches invite people to get underneath the stories they tell to the heart of the matter. Asking supervisees to 'show' the situation they are trying to explore using images, objects, art, music or movement can free them 'from the tunnel of words to find colour, energy, creativity and a sense of mystery which is so often lacking in the practice of supervision'.[12] A supervisor might say: 'Using any of the objects you have in your bag, show me the team you are referring to. Show me that knot in your stomach that you are describing. Show me what losing the thread means. Show me where in your body that feeling resides. Close your eyes and make a sound which expresses that moment you are trying to get me to understand. Choose a card to depict what it was like to be in the chair at that meeting and another to indicate where you would rather have been.' When situations are explored in this way new meaning can emerge in quite surprising ways. This is what Antony Williams calls the 'boo' factor of expressive supervision.[13] Supervisors working with telling approaches need to offer gentle but firm containment since the

---

12 A. Williams, 1995, *Visual and Active Supervision: Roles, Focus, Technique*, New York, London: Norton.

13 Williams, *Visual and Active Supervision*.

unconscious is often accessed quickly and deeply through this manner of exploration. Remaining true to the role of supervisor may involve some delicate negotiation here. Supervisors will also need to be aware that some of their supervisees will be 'act hungry' and relish the opportunity to show their work in this way but be less keen to draw out the implications for action that result from insights gained.

- *Impact here and now.* Every story impacts upon its hearers. Some stories excite us, some bore us. Some intrigue, some capture our imagination, some appal or horrify us. The impact of a story told in supervision provides invaluable information. Social convention allows for certain impacts to be voiced. Stories that generate a 'wow' factor are welcomed, while those that leave us feeling 'yuk' are often left hanging in the air. Feeding back to a supervisee the impact that the particular fragment from their 'then and there' professional story has had on you 'here and now' can be very illuminative. Consider for example a supervisor saying to a supervisee: 'I was totally engrossed by what you were saying, until it flashed through my mind that you might be having me on.' One result would be that the supervisee takes the feedback personally and is offended. If that happened, it could mean that the earlier stage of hosting and containing needs to be revisited. This could be because the supervisor has not paid enough attention to building a relationship conducive to learning or that the supervisor has not pitched their feedback in a way that the supervisee can receive. (It could of course be that the supervisee is feeling particularly vulnerable today for whatever reason.) However, if hosting and containing is secure, and the eliciting and focusing stage has been well handled, then the feedback 'I was totally engrossed by what you were saying until it flashed through my mind that you might be having me on' might stop the supervisee in their tracks and lead them to at least ponder whether the supervisor's experience of being engrossed and duped in rapid succession resonates with their own experience of working with the client or scenario they have presented in supervision. In short, 'exploring the impact' is my laicization of what the therapeutic world handles under the specialized language of transference, countertransference and parallel process.

- *Image and metaphor.* Sometimes the impact of what is presented manifests within those who listen as stray thoughts (must check my bank account to see if she has paid), distractions (wonder what is on TV tonight), images (she looks haunted today) or metaphors (Humpty Dumpty all over again). A supervisor who fails to clear her head and heart to make room for and become truly present to the supervisee before the session began will be disabled by such occurrences and unable to discern whether they arise out of the supervisee's material or from her own lack of presence. Conversely, a supervisor who is ready to greet her guest will know that this strange and apparently random information belongs not to her but to the supervisee and can therefore tentatively offer it for exploration.

- *Somatic resonance.* Strictly speaking somatic resonance is a particular form of communication by impact but I have singled it out in order to accentuate the importance of the supervisor being fully present – including bodily and energetically – to those with whom they work. Thus, for example, a supervisor may suddenly be overwhelmed by tiredness, a tiredness that has no basis in fact since they have slept well and were feeling rested until the supervisee began to speak about their work with a particular client. Feeding back that tiredness as information (without interpretation) is likely to interrupt the narrative and in so doing raise the possibility that something tiring, or energy sapping is going on in the situation being explored or more generally since tiredness is non-verbal, that something is not being said and is not getting through by use of words in the session. When, for example as supervisor, I get a stitch in my side, a sudden stiffness in my neck, sweaty palms, my first task is to ask whether this somatic experience belongs to me or the person I am accompanying. If it belongs to me, then I can note it and park it in order to give X my full attention, but if I am clear that it does not belong to me, then I need to listen very carefully. Does the stiffness intensify or diminish the longer we speak? Does the stitch in my side come and go or remain constant? At some point in the session the time comes for me as supervisor to share what is going on with the supervisee. 'I have had a stitch in my side for the last five minutes. I wonder if that has anything to do with what you are describing.' 'My hands have become increasingly sweaty as I listen to you talking about that meeting. Does that connect with the experience you are describing?' While somatic resonance should not be sought in supervision, neither should it be resisted when it emerges unbidden. Not all supervisors are susceptible to this form of communication by impact, but those who are would do well to monitor this in supervision on supervision.

Tracking and monitoring

Tracking is both a discrete moment in the reflective cycle and a way of monitoring and paying attention to what is happening in the supervisory space as a whole. Tracking has two components:

- charting the progress of the supervisory issue;
- monitoring that what happens within the allotted time by way of exploring and imagining meets the needs of the presenter and does not dissolve into a general discussion of a topic which belongs in a seminar room.

As shown in Figure 5, the five aspects of tracking and monitoring are:

- *Interest.* Something caused the presenter to choose this rather than some other issue to bring to supervision. If the eliciting and focusing stage has been well handled, then it will have become clear why this particular issue is of interest to the supervisee. Monitoring what happens to that interest as the session progresses will help maintain momentum. Similarly, supervisors should track their own interest level, noting when they become more interested and when less so. If supervision is conducted in a group, it is sometimes worth explicitly asking what interests the group in what they are hearing.

Figure 5: Tracking and monitoring

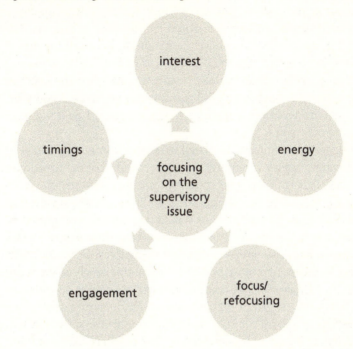

- *Energy.* Tracking energy is closely related to monitoring interest. A loss of energy in supervision may indicate a number of things: that the issue lacked sufficient 'charge' to merit sustained reflection (in which case the option of revising the supervisory question always exists); that loss of energy is a factor in the issue that is currently being presented (a form of parallel process); that the situation carries within it an investment in remaining stuck (for example a client who does not want to get better). As with all interventions, tracking and monitoring energy is best used as a form of noticing or wondering that gives the presenter room to manoeuvre.
- *(Re)Focusing.* A focusing intervention could be along the lines of: 'You said you wanted to explore why you find it so hard to visit the care home. With the group's help you clarified that it was not the care home itself that you found difficult but

having to deal with Molly the manager. When I invited you to show us how you felt when Molly was on duty, you chose the handcuffs, and when I invited you to show us how you felt when she wasn't, you chose the windmill. I noticed the difference in your body energy when you were holding the windmill and when you were holding the handcuffs. For the last five minutes you have been talking about the youth club you visit, and I am wondering if these things are related or if we have gone off track.

- *Engagement.* Supervision is an affair for consenting adults in private. As such it requires engagement. One of the paradoxes of the drive to encourage more widespread take-up of the practice is that some people now come without really being invested in building the relationship that is required or committed to the search for insight aimed at improving their practice. As a consequence, supervisors can find themselves overcompensating and tiring themselves out by doing too much of the work in the session. Ambivalent engagement can also arise when the supervisor or group inadvertently press a button within the psyche or soul of the supervisee causing them to retreat in self-defence. When it becomes clear that this has happened and that the supervisee is not willing to explore that defence within the supervision session, the supervisor has little hope of going any further. In a group setting the supervisor might choose to close the presenter's work at this point and take the remaining time to work with the resonances group members have found in the story originally presented. This will take the spotlight off the presenter allowing them time to regroup and (possibly) re-engage.
- *Timings.* Tracking time relates to safe containment. Simple interventions are helpful here: 'We have an hour together today. I wonder what the best use of that time is for you?'; 'We are halfway through our time together, so I just want to check that we are doing what you need us to do with you today'; 'We have ten minutes left, so I want to ask if you are any closer to finding a way forward?'; 'I am afraid we are now out of time, and there are still unanswered questions, but we do have to

stop there. Thank you.' Another aspect of tracking time is to monitor who is taking the air space and who might not have been able to speak: 'We are halfway through our time, and I notice that we have only heard from three people in the group. Would anyone else like to come in at this point?' or in individual supervision: 'I notice you have spoken continuously for the last thirty minutes and just wonder if you want anything from me before we finish besides a listening ear.'

Bridging and enacting

Figure 6: Bridging and enacting

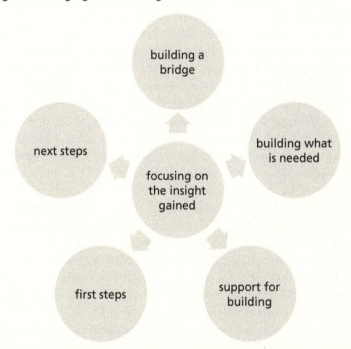

Bridging and enacting are reminders that we reflect on work from the *past*, in the *present* in order to change and enhance work in the *future*. At this stage in the session, we seek to build a bridge from reflection-on-action to the world of everyday practice the supervisee will enter when they leave the session. Enacting is about supervisees articulating first steps expressive of the insight they have found in the session. The literature of coaching offers a great deal of practical insight and wisdom in this area.

- *Building a bridge.* Bridges span two places. Supervisory bridges span the place of exploration and discovery (the supervision session) and the place of enactment (workplace). Just as bridges can be permanent or temporary, made of stone, steel, wood or rope, so too supervisory bridges may be emergency solutions or elaborate constructions which will take many years to complete. However constructed, bridges build professional confidence in helping supervisees recover a sense of empowerment in returning to the workplace.
- *Building what is needed.* Some bridges are built within the supervisee herself. 'I know I can't do anything to change the situation, but knowing that you will be standing there cheering me on from the sidelines already makes a big difference. That is the bridge I am going to hold on to.' Other bridges are conceptual. 'I am going from here today laying down the handcuffs and holding that windmill in my hand. I am going to put a windmill as my screensaver on my computer to remind me what I found here today.' (See p. 208.)
- *Support for building.* Coming as it does at the end of a session this question is deliberately framed positively, 'What will support you?' without the expected rejoinder, 'And what will impede you?' This is partly to do with the supervisory process (the time of exploration has come to an end; we are now in a time of decisive action) and the economy of time (to look at the question from both sides would take longer and impact on the earlier stages in the session). Much more importantly, however, the positive tone of the question is expressive of a philosophical stance which focuses on assets rather than deficits and sees supervisees as highly resourced people capable of making informed choices for themselves. Using the tools of appreciative enquiry, asking what makes for well-being enables the session to end on an empowering note.

- *First steps*. This question is often self-evident, in which case it does not have to be asked. However, if the bridge that has been articulated is overly ambitious, asking about first steps may induce a sense of reality into the equation and therefore save the supervisee from a sense of failure or inadequacy. 'In a few minutes this session will end, and you will leave here to go back to work. What baby step could you take to enact that much bigger desire you have?'
- *Next steps*. Again this is often self-evident. Simple interventions may help. 'You have realized today that you feel inadequate as a counsellor because you haven't kept up with your CPD and have said that even admitting that to me today is a huge first step. So what would your next step be?' … 'And by when will you have done that?'

Reviewing and closing

Reviewing is the process of naming what has been learned through reflection and closing, the drawing of a line on the exploration. In supervision, closing well is just as important as beginning well.

Reviewing works at different levels. In the here and now of the session that is coming to an end, it traces the journey in which both parties have shared from the supervisee's arrival through to their imminent departure. It notes cairns and signposts along the way: that moment of stuckness, the belly laugh that took everyone by surprise; the stray thought which moved things on, the silence that was shared for a few minutes, the moment of connection and so on. Reviewing also works at another level in fostering the supervisee's internal supervisor and reflexivity and in implicitly offering them another tool to use when appropriate with their own clients.

- *Insight gained by supervisee*. Being able to name the learning that has taken place is a key moment in supervision understood as transformational learning. Sometimes insight is crystal clear: 'I am no longer a four-year-old in the playground. Bullies should be resisted.' At other times insight may be embryonic

Figure 7: Reviewing the session

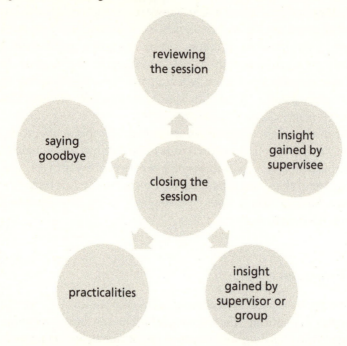

and inarticulate: 'I can't quite put my finger on it, but I know it's something to do with recognizing the difference between caring for my colleagues and being a complete sponge which soaks everything up.' Leaving supervision able to name insight provides a reparative experience for people whose professional lives are often entangled with stories of diminishment of one kind or another.

• *Insight gained by the supervisor or group.* There is an alchemy in supervision that often results in mutual reciprocity: when one person takes the risk of bringing their work to the loving and critically supportive eye of another, both parties benefit from the encounter. In group supervision this is sometimes articulated as follows: 'When one person is supervised every member of the group receives supervision.' Underlying this is the truth that when supervision is conducted within an 'air of hospitality' the truth-telling risk of the presenter evokes (albeit at times unconscious) reflection within the hearers. In group supervision it is good to leave time at the end of the session to invite those present to name any insights gained for their own practice as a result of accompanying the presenter in an exploration of his or her issue. Supervisors need to contain this well lest it turn into grandstanding or competing stories. Insight is what is invited, not storytelling. Even when a group is not present as in individual supervision, it can sometimes be very valuable for supervisees to hear what the supervisor has learned or been reminded of through today's work. Even when it is not appropriate to voice this with supervisees, a hospitable supervisor can note to themselves what gift their guest brought to them today.

- *Practicalities.* Being clear about the date of the next meeting and any expectations involved helps supervisees know that their work lies within an ongoing intentional rather than opportunistic relationship. Dealing with practicalities within the time together always protects leakage into phone calls and emails between sessions and models the kind of containment supervisees would normally be expected to have with their clients.

- *Saying goodbye.* Un-negotiated endings play havoc in people's lives. Many people are drawn to seek help because of unsatisfactory endings: a sudden death, unexpected loss of a job, relationship breakdown, the hanging up of a phone, the slamming of a door. People who have known care as a result of such events often go on to become carers themselves. Supervision offers a chance to model endings that can be healthy, anticipated and negotiated. Managing the micro-endings of each session well will incrementally strengthen the quality of the relationship (for as long as it continues) and play a part in enabling the final goodbye when it comes to an end. As with all aspects of supervision, knowing who you are working with will determine when those goodbyes come. Some supervisees will continue the session right to the front door no matter how many goodbyes you voice. Others know that your standing up implies the session is over and will walk in silence to the door to say goodbye there.

The full cycle of supervision

Figure 8: Typical pattern of supervision session

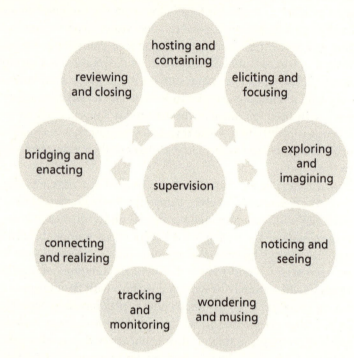

While hosting and containing, eliciting and focusing, exploring and imagining all happen in sequence, noticing and realizing, wondering and musing, connecting and realizing may happen in any order whatsoever as the session progresses.

Similarly, tracking and monitoring take place throughout the session in implicit and explicit ways. Time must be safeguarded to facilitate bridging and enacting, which is crucial to the process of turning insight into action. Reviewing and closing, however brief, close the space and help supervisees return to their daily work once more.

Appendices

This section offers a series of practical material divided into five sections:

1 A definition of pastoral supervision from the Association of Pastoral Supervisors and Educators (APSE).
2 An outline of the three levels of seeing found in John 20.1–9.
3 A practical tool for working with the three levels of seeing within a supervision session.
4 Recommended reading in pastoral supervision.
5 Professional pastoral supervision bodies in the English-speaking world that either foster or offer training in the field.

Appendix 1

A Definition of Pastoral Supervision

Pastoral Supervision is ...
a regular, planned intentional and boundaried space in which a practitioner skilled in supervision (the supervisor) meets with one or more other practitioners (the supervisees) to look together at the supervisees' practice.

a relationship characterized by trust, confidentiality, support and openness that gives the supervisee freedom and safety to explore the issues arising in their work.

spiritually/theologically rich – works within a framework of spiritual/theological understanding in dialogue with the supervisee's world view and work.

psychologically informed – draws on relevant psychological theory and insight to illuminate intra-personal and inter-personal dynamics.

contextually sensitive – pays attention to the particularities of setting, culture and world view.

praxis based – focuses on a report of work and /or issues that arise in and from the supervisee's pastoral practice.

a way of growing in vocational identity, pastoral competence, self-awareness, spiritual/theological reflection, pastoral interpretation, quality of presence, accountability, response to challenge, mutual learning.

attentive to issues of fitness to practice, skill development, management of boundaries, professional identity and the impact of the work upon all concerned parties.

Pastoral Supervision is not ...
Spiritual accompaniment – for the sole or primary purpose of exploring the spiritual life and development of the supervisee(s). Aspects of this may arise in Pastoral Supervision but are not the main focus.

Counselling – for the purpose of helping the supervisee(s) gain insight into their personal dynamics, or helping the supervisee(s) to resolve or live more positively with their psycho-social limitations. Aspects of this may arise in Pastoral Supervision and, if necessary, the supervisee(s) may be encouraged to seek counselling support.

Line management – for the purpose of addressing professional practice and development issues in relationship to the supervisee(s)'s performance and accountability (whether paid or voluntary) to her/his employer. Aspects of this may arise in Pastoral Supervision but are not the main focus.

The Association of Pastoral Supervisors and Educators (APSE), 2008: www.pastoralsupervision.org.uk/

Appendix 2

Three Levels of Seeing

JANE LEACH AND MICHAEL PATERSON

Early on the first day of the week, while it was still dark, Mary Magdalene came to the tomb and saw (blepō) that the stone had been removed from the tomb. ²So she ran and went to Simon Peter and the other disciple, the one whom Jesus loved, and said to them, 'They have taken the Lord out of the tomb, and we do not know where they have laid him.' ³Then Peter and the other disciple set out and went towards the tomb. ⁴The two were running together, but the other disciple outran Peter and reached the tomb first. ⁵He bent down to look in and saw the linen wrappings lying there, but he did not go in. ⁶Then Simon Peter came, following him, and went into the tomb. He saw (theōreō) the linen wrappings lying there, ⁷and the cloth that had been on Jesus' head, not lying with the linen wrappings but rolled up in a place by itself. ⁸Then the other disciple, who reached the tomb first, also went in, and he saw (horaō) and he believed. (John 20.1–8, NRSV)

In the English version of the text, all three kinds of seeing are translated the same: 's/he saw'. But in the Greek the three words used connote different levels of seeing.

1. *Blepō*: First level of seeing. 'I see, I notice.'
    v. 1 Mary notices that the stone has been rolled away.
    v. 5 John notices the linen wrappings lying in the tomb.

2. *Theōreō*: Second level of seeing. 'I wonder, I muse.'
   v. 6 When Simon Peter comes to the tomb, he sees the linen
   wrappings lying there; the cloth from Jesus' head – not with
   the other wrappings but lying separately by itself; rolled up.
   Simon Peter does not just notice these things, but wonders
   about them; he asks how things came to be like this.

3. *horaō*: Third level of seeing. 'I realize, I perceive.'
   v. 9 John goes into the tomb. The verb used refers to a deeper
   level of insight. The spiritual meaning of what he sees is
   emphasized by its coupling with the word, believed: 'He saw
   and believed.' This kind of seeing is about perceiving things as
   they really are; seeing things whole; realizing the truth.

In supervision, supervisors may name what they see or notice,
what arouses curiosity or causes them to wonder, but only supervisees can identify what they realize or perceive as a result of the
reflection.

Appendix 3

Supervisory Interventions

MICHAEL PATERSON

In Chapter 13 I outlined the cyclical structure of a supervision session. Here I offer a tool for exploring the material supervisees bring to supervision based on the three levels of seeing drawn from John 20 outlined in Appendix 2.

First level of seeing – seeing and noticing

The first level of seeing works with the incontrovertible, the facts of the matter, the kind of thing CCTV would pick up, if a supervision session were recorded and played back:

- I notice that today you are clutching on to that cushion.
- I notice that we are only four minutes into our time together, and you have already named many issues, any one of which could fill the hour.
- I notice that I cannot get a word in edgeways today.
- I notice that you told that story without pausing for breath.
- I notice that you haven't made eye contact with me since you started talking about J.
- I notice I am fidgeting more than normal.
- I can normally follow what you are saying, but today I notice I am losing the plot.
- I notice a flatness in your voice today that is not normally there.

Figure 1: Seeing and noticing

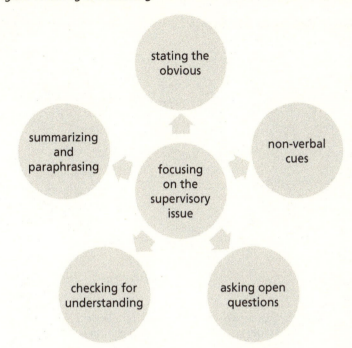

Sometimes supervisors neglect this level of seeing since it appears to be too simple and offends their need to appear sophisticated. In reality being able to state the obvious can result in a breakthrough of insight for the supervisee. See the example in Chapter 12 when in group supervision someone noticed that Mary, a hospice chaplain, ended all her conversations with 'see you later' rather than 'goodbye'. That insight became transformative in helping Mary to realize that her concerns about her partner's health were preventing her from hearing issues of loss and death in her work with dying patients and had led her to become emotionally unavailable to those in her care.

Second level of seeing – wondering and musing

Figure 2: Wondering and musing

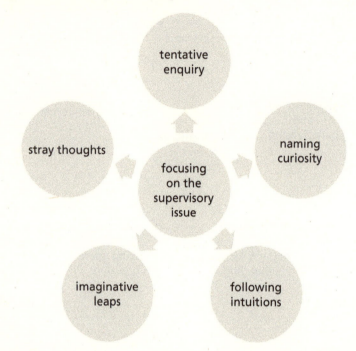

The second level of seeing focuses on whatever arouses curiosity. Stories provoke our imagination and cause us to wonder and to turn things over in our minds.

- I wonder how you got through that awful situation you have just told me about.
- I wonder what supports you from the inside when you work with distress like that.
- I am really curious about your throwaway remark 'that's men for you'.
- I find myself wondering what 'good enough' work is for you.
- I wonder who taught you to be hard on yourself.
- If you had a magic wand, I wonder what you would wish for.

- I wonder what your dream job would be, since you find this one so difficult.
- If ethics didn't prohibit it, what would you really like to do or say to X?
- I wonder what a professionally permitted response to x could be.

Wondering is not the same as analysing or interpreting. Within the overarching context of hospitality, wonderings need to be treated as offerings that supervisees are entirely free to pick up and run with or discard. Supervisors need to pitch their wonderings and musings in ways that open and enlarge space for exploration rather than close and shut it down. The cleverer an interpretation in a supervisor's head is, the less likely it is to be of use to a supervisee. Wondering allows spaciousness to grow within the supervisee's frames of reference. Interpretation tells them what they should have been thinking about. The subtle difference is important, if supervision is to be about transformative learning and not about coming to an expert for a diagnosis and prescription.

Third level of seeing – connecting and realizing

The third level of seeing focuses on making connections between self and work, values and wisdom. It looks for insight, for the penny to drop, for things to fall into place, the fog to lift and clarity to dawn. Realizing the significance of the part within the whole is the whole raison d'être of supervision. While exploring things for their own sake may be intellectually stimulating, unless it results in insightful ways to improve future practice, it will be of limited value. What Parker Palmer says of education can also be said of supervision: 'space needs to be charged'.[1] The 'charge' running through supervision is the commitment to ensure that those on the receiving end of the supervisee's care receive the best deal possible.

---

1 P. J. Palmer, 1998, *The Courage to Teach*, San Francisco: Jossey-Bass, pp. 73–7.

Figure 3: Connecting and realizing

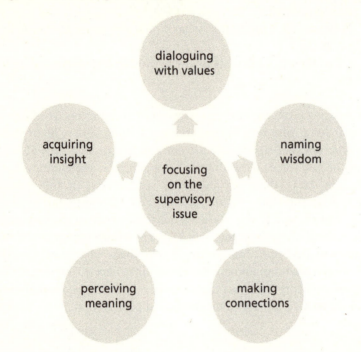

- How does what you are describing connect with your value system?
- What do you realize about the values of the organization you are working within?
- What are the internal stories that give you meaning and purpose?
- How does this piece of work connect to your own sources of wisdom?
- What throws you off balance in your work?
- Where do you find your equilibrium?
- What is the worst that could happen ... the best that could happen?
- What do you realize by engaging this little story with the macro stories of your practice, life, spiritual tradition?

Appendix 4

Recommended Reading in Supervision and Reflective Practice

Readers may wish to follow up some of the texts that are referred to in the footnotes for each chapter. Some more general reading is suggested below.

Supervisory frameworks

A. Davys and L. Beddoe, 2010, *Best Practice in Professional Supervision: A Guide for the Helping Professions*, London: Jessica Kingsley.

P. Hawkins and R. Shohet, 2012, *Supervision in the Helping Professions*, 4th edn, Maidenhead: Open University Press.

F. Inskipp and B. Proctor, 1993, *The Art, Craft and Tasks of Counselling Supervision*, Twickenham: Cascade Publications.

S. Page and V. Wosket, 1994, *Supervising the Counsellor: A Cyclical Model*, London: Routledge.

S. Ryan, 2004, *Vital Practice: Stories from the Healing Arts, the Homeopathic and Supervisory Way*, Portland, OR: Sea Change.

Supervision, spirituality and ministry

M. Carroll, 2001, 'The Spirituality of Supervision', in M. Carroll and M. Tholstrup (eds), *Integrative Approaches to Supervision*, London and Philadelphia: Jessica Kingsley.

W. R. DeLong, 2010, *Courageous Conversations: The Teaching and Learning of Pastoral Supervision*, Lanham, ML: University Press of America.

J. Foskett and D. Lyall, 1988, *Helping the Helpers: Supervision in Pastoral Care*, London: SPCK.

C. Hunter, 2003, 'Supervised Theological Field Education: A Phenomenological Inquiry', Doctor of Ministry Studies thesis, Melbourne: Melbourne College of Divinity.

C. Hunter, 2006, 'One Small Step: Creative Art and the Art of Supervision for Ministry', *Reflective Practice: Formation and Supervision in Ministry* 26, pp. 133–48.

J. Leach and M. Paterson, 2010, *Pastoral Supervision: A Handbook*, London: SCM Press.

J. Neafsey, 2005, 'Seeing Beyond: A Contemplative Approach to Supervision', in M. R. Bumpus and R. B. Langer (eds), 2005, *Supervision of Spiritual Directors: Engaging in Holy Mystery*, Harrisburg, PA: Morehouse Publishing, pp. 17–31.

S. Miller, 2007, *Keeping It Together: A Reflective Practice Tool for Faith-Based Community Development Practitioners*, London: Faith Based Regeneration Network Publishers.

M. Paterson, 2013, 'Mirror Mirror on the Wall: From Reflection to Transformative Practice', *Journal of Health and Social Care Chaplaincy* 1:1, pp. 67–74.

M. Paterson and E. Kelly, 2013, 'Values-based Reflective Practice: A Method Developed in Scotland for Spiritual Care Practitioners', *Practical Theology* 6:1, pp. 51–68.

K. Pohly, 2001, *Transforming the Rough Places: The Ministry of Supervision*, 2nd edn, Franklin, TN: Providence House.

H. Richardson, 2009, 'A Musical Metaphor for Pastoral Supervision', *Practical Theology* 2:3, pp. 373–86.

J. Rose, 2013, *Psychology for Pastoral Contexts: A Handbook*, London: SCM Press.

H. Smith and M. K. Smith, 2008, *The Art of Helping Others: Being Around, Being There, Being Wise*, London: Jessica Kingsley.

B. Whorton, 2011, *Reflective Caring: Imaginative Listening to Pastoral Experience*, London: SPCK.

Supervision as transformative learning

M. Carroll, 2009, 'Supervision: Critical Reflection for Trans-formational Learning, Part 1', *The Clinical Supervisor* 28:2, pp. 210–20.

M. Carroll, 2010, 'Levels of Reflection: On Learning Reflection', *Psychotherapy in Australia* 16:2, pp. 28–35.

M. Carroll and M. Gilbert, 2011, *On Being a Supervisee: Creating Learning Partnerships*, 2nd edn, London: Vukani Publishing.

J. Mezirow, 1991, *Transformative Dimensions of Adult Learning*, San Francisco: Jossey-Bass.

R. Shohet (ed.), 2008, *Passionate Supervision*, London: Jessica Kingsley.

R. Shohet (ed.), 2011, *Supervision as Transformation: A Passion for Learning*, London and Philadelphia: Jessica Kingsley.

N. Weld, 2012, *A Practical Guide to Transformative Supervision for the Helping Professions: Amplifying Insight*, London: Jessica Kingsley.

Group supervision

E. Hillerbrand, 1989, 'Cognitive Differences between Experts and Novices: Implications for Group Supervision', *Journal of Counseling and Development* 67:5, pp. 293–6.

E. L. Holloway and R. Johnston, 1985, 'Group Supervision: Widely Practiced But Poorly Understood', *Counselor Education and Supervision* 24:4, pp. 332–40.

F. McDermott, 2003, *Inside Group Work: A Guide to Reflective Practice*, Melbourne: Allen & Unwin.

S. Page and V. Wosket, 1994, *Supervising the Counsellor: A Cyclical Model*, London: Routledge, pp. 158–79.

B. Proctor, 2008, *Group Supervision: A Guide to Creative Practice*, 2nd edn, London: Sage.

Organizational supervision

M. Carroll, 2001, 'Supervision in and for organizations', in M. Carroll and M. Tholstrup (eds), 2001, *Integrative Approaches to Supervision*, London and Philadelphia: Jessica Kingsley, pp. 50–64.

A. Davys and L. Beddoe, 2010, *Best Practice in Professional Supervision: A Guide for the Helping Professions*, London: Jessica Kingsley, pp. 69–87.

L. Hughes and P. Pengelly, 1997, *Staff Supervision in a Turbulent Environment*, London: Jessica Kingsley.

J. Pritchard (ed.), 1995, *Good Practice in Supervision: Statutory and Voluntary Organisations*, London: Jessica Kingsley.

N. Weld, 2012, *A Practical Guide to Transformative Supervision for the Helping Professions: Amplifying Insight*, London: Jessica Kingsley, pp. 81–98.

Journaling and creative writing

G. Bolton, 2005, *Reflective Practice: Writing and Professional Development*, Thousand Oaks, CA: Sage.

J. Moon and J. Fowler, 2008, 'There is a Story to be Told: A Framework for the Conception for Story in Higher Education and Professional Development', *Nurse Education Today* 28:2, pp. 232–9.

J. Moon, 2004, *A Handbook of Reflective and Experiential Practice*, Abingdon: Routledge.

Creative approaches

A. Chesner and L. Zografou, 2013, *Creative Supervision across Modalities*, London: Jessica Kingsley.

N. Hartley and M. Payne, 2008, *The Creative Arts in Palliative Care*, London: Jessica Kingsley.

M. Lahad, 2000, *Creative Supervision: The Use of Expressive Arts in Supervision and Self-Supervision*, London: Jessica Kingsley.

C. Schuck and J. Wood, 2011, *Inspiring Creative Supervision*, London: Jessica Kingsley.

Rachel Verney and Gary Ansdell, 2010, 'Conversation 8: On Teaching and Supervising Music Therapists', in *Conversations on Nordorff–Robbins Music Therapy*, Gilsum, NH: Barcelona Publishers, pp. 71–84.

A. Williams, 1995, *Visual and Active Supervision: Roles, Focus, Technique*, London: Norton.

Ethical issues

BACP, 2010, *Ethical Framework for Good Practice in Counselling and Psychotherapy*, Lutterworth: BACP: www.bacp.co.uk

UKCP Ethical Principles and Code of Conduct: www.psycho therapy.org.uk

J. Dewane, 2007, 'Supervisor, Beware: Ethical Dangers in Supervision', *Social Work Today* 7:4, p. 34 – www.socialworktoday. com/archive/julyaug2007p34.shtml

J. E. Falvey and C. R. Cohen, 2004, 'The Buck Stops Here', *The Clinical Supervisor* 22:2, pp. 63–80.

G. Leonard and J. Beazley Richards, 2001, 'How Supervisors Can Protect Themselves from Complaints and Litigation', in M. Carroll and M. Tholstrup (eds), *Integrative Approaches to Supervision*, London: Jessica Kingsley.

S. Page and V. Wosket, 1994, *Supervising the Counsellor: A Cyclical Model*, London: Routledge, pp. 180–203.

Power in supervision

C. Barstow, 2008, *Right Use of Power: The Heart of Ethics: A Resource for the Helping Professional*, Boulder, CO: Many Realms Publishing.

H. Dhillon-Stevens, 2001, 'Anti-oppressive Practice in the Supervisory Relationship', in M. Carroll and M. Tholstrup (eds), *Integrative Approaches to Supervision*, London: Jessica Kingsley, pp. 155–63.

A. Guggenbuhl-Craig, 1971, *Power in the Helping Professions*, Woodstock: Spring Publications.

E. Holloway, 1998, 'Power in the Supervisory Relationship', Keynote Address, British Association of Supervision Practice and Research Conference, London.

M. J. Murphy and D. W. Wright, 2005, 'Supervisees' Perspectives of Power Use in Supervision', *Journal of Marital and Family Therapy* 31:3, pp. 283–95.

S. Page and V. Wosket, 1994, *Supervising the Counsellor: A Cyclical Model*, London: Routledge, pp. 204–28.

N. Sims, 2008, 'Power and Supervision in the Context of the Church and its Ministry', *Practical Theology* 1:2, pp. 203–17.

Professional identity

C. Clegg, 2011, 'Pastoral Supervision: Ministry, Spirit and Regulation', in L. Bondi, D. Carr, C. Clark and C. Clegg, *Towards Professional Wisdom: Practical Deliberation in the People Professions*, Farnham: Ashgate, pp. 219–31.

E. Kelly, 2012, *Personhood and Presence: Self as a Resource for Spiritual and Pastoral Care*, London: Continuum.

The self of the supervisor

I. Renzenbrink, 2011, *Caregiver Stress and Staff Support in Illness, Dying and Bereavement*, Oxford: Oxford University Press.

T. M. Skovholt and M. H. Ronnestad, 1995, *The Evolving Professional Self*, Chichester: Wiley.

L. van Dernoot Lipsky, 2009, *Trauma Stewardship: An Everyday Guide to Caring for Self While Caring for Others*, San Francisco: Berrett-Koehler Publishers.

V. Wosket, 1999, *The Therapeutic Use of Self: Counselling Practice, Research and Supervision*, London: Routledge.

Values-based practice

K. W. M. Fulford and K. Woodbridge, 'Values-based Practice: Help and Healing within a Shared Theology of Diversity', in M. E. Coyte, P. Gilbert, V. Nicholls (eds), *Spirituality, Values and Mental Health: Jewels for the Journey*, London: Jessica Kingsley.

S. Kahan, 2008, 'Creating Value-based Competition in Health Care', *Essays on Issues. The Federal Reserve Bank of Chicago*, September, No. 254a.

E. Kelly, 2013, 'Translating Theological Reflective Practice into Values Based Reflection: A Report from Scotland', *Reflective Practice: Formation and Supervision in Ministry* 33, pp. 246–56.

P. M. Lencioni, 2002, 'Make Your Values Mean Something', *Harvard Business Review* (July), pp. 113–17.

J. M. Little, 2002, 'Humanistic Medicine or Values-based Medicine: What's in a Name?', *Medical Journal of Australia* 177:6, pp. 319–21.

M. Petrova, J. Dale and B. Fulford, 2006, 'Values-based Practice in Primary Care: Easing the Tensions between Individual Values, Ethical Principles and Best Evidence', *British Journal of General Practice* 56:530, pp. 703–9.

J. Rose, 2002, *Sharing Spaces? Prayer and the Counselling Relationship*, London: Darton, Longman & Todd.

B. Thorne, 1998, 'Values and Spirituality at Work', *Counselling at Work* 21, pp. 3–4.

Developmental stages in supervision

T. M. Bear and D. M. Kivlighan, 1994, 'Single Subject Examination of the Process of Supervision of Beginning and Advanced

Supervisees', *Professional Psychology: Research and Practice* 25:4, pp. 450–7.

J. Chagnon and R. K. Russell, 1995, 'Assessment of Supervisee Developmental Level and Supervision Environment across Supervisor Experience', *Journal of Counseling and Development* 73:5, pp. 553–8.

J. Leach and M. Paterson, 2010, *Pastoral Supervision: A Handbook*, London: SCM Press, pp. 93–8.

Appendix 5

Professional Bodies and Training in Pastoral Supervision

Association of Pastoral Supervisors and Educators (UK)

The Association of Pastoral Supervisors and Educators (APSE) exists to promote high standards of pastoral supervision by providing a system of accreditation for pastoral supervisors and educators in pastoral supervision; supporting initiatives in the training of pastoral supervisors; fostering groups for the support, accountability and continuing development of pastoral supervisors and encouraging conversation among the various traditions and contexts of pastoral supervision and pastoral supervision education.
www.pastoralsupervision.org.uk

Institute of Pastoral Supervision and Reflective Practice (UK)

The Institute of Pastoral Supervision and Reflective Practice (IPSRP) is a community of advanced practitioners committed to training, research and publishing. Members of the Institute offer training across the UK from taster events and skills workshops to professional diploma-level courses in pastoral supervision and reflective practice.
www.ipsrp.org.uk

Supervisors Association of Ireland

The Supervisors Association of Ireland (SAI) is a learning community which seeks to promote cross-professional supervision. SAI's commitments are to promote a code of ethics and discipline among its members; to develop high standards of practice in supervision and training for supervision and to respond to ongoing developmental needs and research within the area of supervisory practice through support, networking, workshops, conferences and publications.
www.saivision.ie

Transforming Practices (Australia)

Transforming Practices is a group of autonomous practitioners who foster personal and social transformation through skilled practices in adult education, mediation, spiritual direction, counselling and professional and pastoral supervision. Practitioners are recognized supervisors with the Australasian Association of Supervision (AAOS) as well as other relevant professional associations. Transforming Practices offers training in supervision.
www.transformingpractices.com.au

College of Pastoral Supervision and Psychotherapy (USA)

The College of Pastoral Supervision and Psychotherapy is a theologically based covenant community, dedicated to 'Recovery of Soul'. CPSP offers accredited training in pastoral psychotherapy, pastoral supervision, pastoral counselling and clinical chaplaincy.
www.pastoralreport.com